Making Quality Happen

Making Quality Happen

A STEP BY STEP GUIDE TO WINNING THE QUALITY REVOLUTION

Roderick M. McNealy

Director of Customer Driven Quality at Johnson & Johnson
Health Care Systems Inc.
New Jersey, USA

CHAPMAN & HALL

London · Glasgow · New York · Tokyo · Melbourne · Madras

Published by Chapman & Hall, 2–6 Boundary Row, London SE1 8HN

Chapman & Hall, 2–6 Boundary Row, London SE1 8HN, UK

Blackie Academic & Professional, Wester Cleddens Road, Bishopbriggs, Glasgow G64 2NZ, UK

Chapman & Hall Inc., 29 West 35th Street, New York NY10001, USA

Chapman & Hall Japan, Thomson Publishing Japan, Hirakawacho Nemoto Building, 6F, 1–7–11 Hirakawa-cho, Chiyoda-ku, Tokyo 102, Japan

Chapman & Hall Australia, Thomas Nelson Australia, 102 Dodds Street, South Melbourne, Victoria 3205, Australia

Chapman & Hall India, R. Seshadri, 32 Second Main Road, CIT East, Madras 600 035, India

First edition 1993
Reprinted 1996
First published in paperback 1996

© 1993 Roderick M. McNealy

Typeset in Times 11/13pts by Mews Photosetting, Beckenham, Kent
Printed in Great Britain by TJ Press, Padstow, Cornwall

ISBN 0 412 55310 4

A catalogue record for this book is available from the British Library

Library of Congress Cataloging-in-Publication data available

Contents

CONTENTS

Foreword

Customer-focused Quality has never been more important than it is today. In the intensely competitive global business environment of the 1990s and beyond, all consumers are looking for greater value. Every type of organization must be increasingly efficient and effective in providing this value, or they risk losing their place in the market. Firmly established organizations with outstanding reputations for products and services are finding their worlds turned 'upside down', as the needs of their customers and their markets change and they are either slow to respond or unwilling to do so. Conversely, organizations focused on addressing customers needs and desires in specialized niche markets – long neglected by larger organizations – are enjoying remarkable growth, vitality, and profitability.

This is not occurring by random chance or luck. Those organizations – in any industry – that are focused on addressing the needs of their customers are going to be able to provide goods and services that address those needs and do so more rapidly than organizations who have lost touch with their customers. If an organization is in close contact with its customers – working almost in a partnership – it will inevitably be more efficient because it is focusing on their needs and desires. It is not wasting or misappropriating its resources on irrelevant or insignificant enterprises of no interest to the customer.

Customer focus has been the basis for much of the effort involved in the Quality process. In fact, this customer focus and Quality itself have been referred to as 'common sense' practices that any organization should follow. Customer focus and Quality may be common sense, but few organizations actually practice these basic fundamentals of good management. Those who do are noteworthy in their success.

In *Making Quality Happen* Rod McNealy has made these common sense practices easily understood, feasible and practical. His presentation is not one of a new theory or new approach to Quality, but rather an implementation discussion targeted at those organizations that really want to **do** something about Quality and to focus on their customers rather than merely **talk** about doing so. Moreover, *Making Quality Happen* presents this information in an easily understood, yet action-oriented fashion. The reader is not left with that 'this is interesting, but how do I do it' feeling so common with organizational issues such as Quality. The step by step approach is logical and easy to follow. *Making Quality Happen* is a book any organization can utilize to improve and it can be a ready reference to revisit when we are tempted to stray from our Customer focus.

Christopher Forbes
Vice Chairman, Forbes Magazine
New York
April, 1993

Introduction

Quality is the single most important issue confronting America and American industry. The future of our economic system, and thus our nation, is directly tied to our ability as a nation, as an industrial force, and as individual managers and employees within that industrial network, to produce goods and services which meet the ever-changing demands of the expanding world marketplace.

In fact, the situation is exactly comparable for Western European nations as they face the prospect of a unified European economy. How will each nation be able to differentiate its products and services – and thus economically survive – in this new market environment? Moreover, how will the developing economies of Eastern Europe be able to establish a marketplace 'foothold' and survive? How can they hope to compete against the established economic powerhouses of Germany, France, and Britain? Quality can be their most important strategic weapon in the economic revolution overtaking Europe.

Yet Quality is a subject that is often veiled in vague generalities and shrouded by imprecise terms such as 'excellence' and 'perfection'. However, it is vital to the future success of American and European industries, and all their managers and employees, that Quality be understood as a specific, clearly defined, and universally applied subject. The purpose of this book is to provide that needed clarity by answering the three most basic and frequently asked questions concerning the issue of Quality and Quality Improvement. These three questions are 'why?', 'what?', and 'how?'

These three general questions quickly lead to several other, more specific, questions:

'Why should I be interested in Quality and Quality Improvement?'

'Why do I, personally, need to get involved?'

'What is Quality and, specifically, what is Quality Improvement?'

'What do *I* have to gain from Quality?'

'What will my world look like if I do get involved with Quality Improvement?'

'What is the real "bottom line" financial impact of Quality?'

'How do I make Quality happen?'

Each of these questions is invariably asked by anyone confronted by the subject of Quality and considering the issue of Quality Improvement. This book will answer each of these questions with an emphasis on practical application.

Quality as addressed by this book is not a theoretical subject nor will Quality Improvement be discussed in vague conceptual terms. Rather, a specific plan will be presented for understanding the vital importance of Quality to the Business World of today and for implementing Quality Improvement into organizations of any type and size, regardless of geographic location.

The goal of this book is to enable an individual to understand Quality, realize the need for Quality Improvement, and become excited by the tremendous potential and opportunity represented by improving the Quality of every facet of any organization. *Making Quality Happen* will benefit our country, our companies, and each of us as individuals.

For my wife Patricia and my two daughters
Mary Kathleen and Rebecca Ann for all their support
and understanding

Why Quality?

Why should we be interested in Quality and concern ourselves with Quality Improvement? In particular, why should an organization's top management devote any of its valuable time to a subject which is already the supposed responsibility of employees in Quality Assurance and Quality Control? On the surface, it appears American industry is at least as powerful as ever. What other nation has landed men on the moon, built companies such as those in the FORTUNE 500, and produced an economy that employs 112 440 000 people and produces $4527 billion in goods and services [1]?

Certainly, Quality cannot be that big a problem. Possibly it is not that important after all. Why tinker with success?

In sharp contrast to this reasoning stands the cold, harsh reality of our current national deficits in both the Balance of Trade and the Balance of Payments. The Balance of Trade deficit for the United States in 1990 is $108.7 billion. This figure represents 'the net amount of exports less imports' [2] for 1990. At the same time, our total Balance of Payments – 'the total flow of money payments, such as foreign investment, loans, and other cash flows, as well as payments for goods and services' [3] – stands at a deficit of $99.3 billion.

Considering these numbers in a vacuum can be misleading. Rather, they must be viewed in context, and in this case, seen in relation to recent trends for these figures. A review of the recent Balance of Trade and Balance of Payments results provides a clearer indication of exactly what the current figures represent, as we see in Fig. 1.1.

Quite simply, these two indicators categorically demonstrate that both the United States and foreign populations are increasingly likely

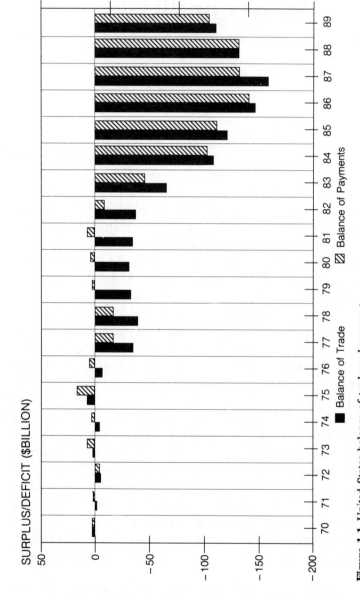

SURPLUS/DEFICIT ($BILLION)

Figure 1.1 United States balance of trade and payments.
This chart provides an historical trend of United States Balance of Trade and Balance of Payments surpluses and deficits for the period 1969–1989.
'Source: United States Bureau of the Census.'

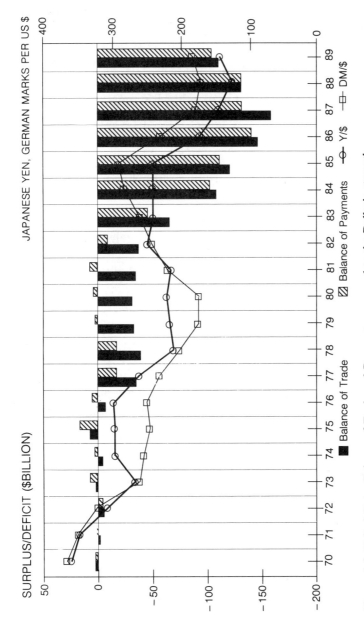

Figure 1.2 United States Balance of Trade and Payments compared to the Dollar's strength.
This chart compares the trend of United States Balance of Trade and Balance of Payments surpluses and deficits for the period 1969–1989 with the strength of the Dollar versus the Japanese Yen and German Mark during the same period.
'Source: United States Bureau of the Census.'

to purchase goods and services produced by other nations than those produced in the United States. Moreover, the trends for both numbers show this deficit trend moderating only slightly.

Some will say the deficits are tied to, or at least influenced by, the strength of the US dollar. Within recent memory, we have all heard economists and commentators intone, 'If the dollar weakens versus the Japanese YEN or German MARK then American goods will be more attractive to foreign markets, thereby reducing the deficit.'

In fact, the Dollar has been 'weak' and 'strong' within the past few years and the worst trade deficits have occurred during the periods of its greatest relative weakness, as seen in Fig. 1.2.

Thus, emphasis on the dollar's relative strength or weakness merely represents our concentration on a possible symptom of the problem, not the real cause. Possibly, this is because the real cause of our deficits is too painful to contemplate. Simply put, our own citizens are less interested in, have less confidence in, and are therefore less likely to buy American made products than those made elsewhere.

The longer term outgrowth of the Balance of Payments trend is ominous. Foreign competitors become increasingly powerful as more and more business flows to them and away from their US counter-parts. Companies in the US are then more susceptible to acquisition by foreign held companies now flushed with working capital and confident management.

A leading example of this trend can be seen in the advertising industry which is now dominated by British-run conglomerates. In fact, two of the top three advertising agencies in the US (J. Walter Thompson Company and Saatchi and Saatchi) are British controlled. Currently, British-run advertising firms control 31.6% of the total advertising billings for the top 50 advertising agencies in the US. They represented 5% only 5 years ago [4]. It is somewhat startling to consider the prospect of an industry so intimately involved with shaping and monitoring the wants, needs, and feelings of the American population being directed by individuals who are not even part of that population.

4

Or, if we move from Madison Avenue to money management and the American banking industry, we find a similar situation. Currently, seven of the ten largest banks in the world are Japanese, the other three are French. Ten years ago the largest bank in the world was American, eight of the ten largest were European, and there were no Japanese banks among the world's ten largest [5]. It was incomprehensible that American and European financial dominance would ever be challenged. Totally inconceivable. The US and Europe were banking. These were the nations of J.P. Morgan, the Rothschilds, the Rockefellers, Bernard Baruch, the Bank of England, Barclays, the Bank of America.

Therefore, at least the American banking industry believed it could make high risk loans to third world countries, underwrite poorly conceived, carelessly managed ventures in the US, all the while paying their depositors 5% on passbook savings accounts, opening at 10 am and closing at 2.30 pm. No Saturday hours, thank you very much.

Moreover, the savings and loan industry, which in the deregulated financial world competes on many levels with traditional banking, has proven to be more than the equal of the larger banking establishments when it comes to incompetence, greed, and short-term, short-sighted management. This management has now presented the American people with a bill for $183 billion [6] which we are asked to pay and be grateful for. In fact, this is merely a larger version of numerous other defective goods and services which we are provided on a daily basis and expected to cheerfully pay for.

Our tendency is to stand back, observe these events and either be overwhelmed by their enormity or be indifferent to their implications on our lives. Yet, these and similar events have a direct bearing and impact on our lives and a nation's future.

For example, a weakened savings and loan industry, or a foreign controlled banking system, may be far less responsive to the needs of the domestic US economy. Specifically, funds may not be available for housing, schools, small and mid-sized industry. This can occur if the managers of our financial resources are underwriting foreign investments or providing capital to larger American firms

5

increasingly less able to generate sufficient funds internally due to decreasing market share and sales.

Is all of this inevitable?

If a 'weak' or 'strong' dollar will not solve our Balance of Payments and Balance of Trade dilemmas, what will? What is the formula for rebuilding the American economy to its former prominence and re-establishing control over our own destiny? How will the established economies of the newly unified Europe prosper and the neo-natal free market economies of Eastern Europe survive?

QUALITY

It is really quite simple. If American and European industries produce goods and services which meet customers' needs, and if these goods and services provide value to that customer, then the US will return to its former position in the world market, Western European nations will prosper, and Eastern European economies will survive. If we are 'customer-driven', so that all our efforts are outwardly focused on our customers and in serving them, then we will succeed.

However, being 'customer driven' will involve a dramatic shift from the current inwardly directed focus predominating American and many European industries. This current direction emphasizes quarter to quarter profits at the expense of long term goals and rewards crisis management rather than prevention and proactive planning.

Wall Street stock market analysts have become the 'customer' for many US companies. At one time, Wall Street acted merely as a 'score keeper', recording and reflecting the financial results of a firm's marketplace endeavors. However, that role has changed dramatically in that Wall Street is now an active 'player' in the marketplace with direct impact and influence on the day to day operations of organizations.

This new role has developed based upon the large institutional fund holdings in world markets. These large institutional funds succeed or fail based upon their ability to generate the results they have forecast for their customers. These forecasts, in turn, are

6

based upon earnings projections for various industries as developed by analysts employed by these funds. Therefore, it is quite possible, and is in fact a frequent occurrence, that individual organizations may show excellent growth versus comparable year ago periods, yet not achieve the specific levels forecast by market analysts. This can result in sharp stock price fluctuations, increased pressure on senior management for short term actions, and a diversion of attention from the long term, customer focus that remains an organization's best hope for real marketplace success.

Accordingly, all corporate energies are now channelled toward pleasing these analysts rather than the real customer for our goods and services.

Because the required shift in management cultures, from the current inwardly focused style to the required outwardly focused one, is so dramatic and far reaching, it is necessary to expand upon the reasons for such a change. Certainly, management is unlikely to change established habits in the absence of a clearly perceived need to do so.

Remember that Captain Edward J. Smith, with 38 years of sailing experience in the North Atlantic, failed to heed four distinct iceberg warnings as he drove the *Titanic* at full speed into an ice field on that 'night to remember' in April 1912 [7].

Or that George Armstrong Custer, a brevet general at the age of 26 and a celebrated American Civil War hero, and accompanied by his brother Tom, a hero in his own right who had earned two Congressional Medals of Honor, disregarded the warnings of seasoned and battle hardened Indian scouts when he led his 7th Cavalry regiment of 150 men against a Sioux encampment of 6000 warriors along the Little Bighorn River.

Some will just not believe a crisis is at hand.

To some, the national deficits we just discussed may be too 'long term' in nature, too global in scope to really impact their day to day habits. Therefore we must examine four other distinct reasons why Quality is so vital, why now is the time for 'making quality happen'.

These four reasons can be categorized under the subject areas of:

COMPETITION
CONSTERNATION
COSTS
CARING

Competition

Tom Peters, the author of *Thriving on Chaos, In Search of Excellence*, and numerous other books on Quality and industry, has stated that the period from 1946 to 1974 was the 'Great American Winning Streak'. This occurred only because American corporations faced no significant foreign competition during this period. Peters emphasizes this point by stating that it was impossible to 'screw up' a FORTUNE 500 company from 1946 to 1974, 'even if you tried' – and many did – merely because the international business climate was just so favorable to American industry.

This has all changed dramatically in the last 15 years. Unfortunately, most managements have not recognized the new competitive

"Unless I'm misinterpreting the signs, gentlemen, we are approaching the end of the golden age of shoddy merchandise."

Drawing by Weber: 1983 The New Yorker Magazine Inc.

environment and even among those that have, few have aggressively responded to it.

For example, take the simple lawn-mower. Ask any number of people – and our sample totalled 3000 – what the most difficult part about mowing their lawn is and they will answer 'starting the mower' over 90% of the time. Market researchers call this level of response 'statistically significant'. Consumers call it 'blindingly obvious'.

Next, we need to consider the players in the lawn-mower game. They read like a family album – John Deere ('nothing runs like a Deere'); Toro; Snapper; Lawn Boy; Sears. The vast majority of these mowers are powered by engines from Briggs and Stratton, manufactured in Milwaukee, Wisconsin – America's 'Heartland'.

Lawn-mowers. As American as apple pie and a cool glass of lemonade after cutting through the front yard.

However, we now need to ask what is the most highly rated lawn-mower, as ranked by Consumers Union, publishers of *Consumers Reports*. And which mower has held, or shared, this distinction since its introduction in 1978?

HONDA

Because the Japanese have so much lawn to mow. Japan, where landscaping means rock gardens and whose idea of trees – the bonsai – looks like an arboreal Yoda and stands in sharp contrast to the American Redwood. How did this happen?

HONDA listened

They listened to the American consumer. When Honda experienced excess capacity in small motorcycle engines, market research was conducted to more clearly understand what appliances and products used similar engines and what were the customer likes and dislikes about each of these products. Basic, straightforward market research. Talk to your customer, ask the right questions, and then listen. And learn.

HONDA learned

They learned the exact same lesson we discovered in our 3000 interviews. Existing power lawn-mowers were hard to start and they needed to be re-started whenever the bagging models had to be

9

emptied. We can all picture in our minds the 'Universal Male' pulling, tugging, cursing, sweating as he vainly attempts to yank the magic starting cord with just the right combination of power and snap to resume the drudgery of our national love affair with our lawns. (Interestingly, Americans spend $1.7 billion on feeding their lawns each year, or approximately $58.00 per household. Certain African nations, such as Somalia, average only $170 per capita for Gross National Product per year.)

HONDA leapfrogged market technology

Lawn-mower manufacturers were content with a technology – dominated by Briggs and Stratton – that produced a mower that would start 'within three pulls'. They even advertised this fact.

However, Honda realized they could not hope to compete in this uniquely American market, dominated by household names, with merely a 'me-too' product – even one that started within two pulls. Therefore, they did not seek to rework the existing technology, but rather to replace it. They accomplished this by incorporating the blade-break clutch and overhead valve engine into their mower. This produced a mower which starts easily on the first pull and Honda used this ease of starting to differentiate themselves from their American competitors in their advertising.

The Honda lawn-mower example also puts to rest a frequently perpetrated myth that low cost Japanese products are 'flooding' the American market. In fact, the Honda lawn-mower is premium priced, whereas the cheapest machines are American made. Importantly, Honda's sales trends clearly demonstrate that the consumer will happily pay a premium price for Quality – for products which meet customers' needs and do so consistently.

Companies competing in the lawn-mower category fell into a prevalent trap in Post-War industry. They had become inwardly focused, enraptured with their internal processes and engulfed in maximizing the efficiency of these processes. Nothing wrong with that – if these processes are producing what your customer really wants. In this case, those internal processes were out of touch with reality and that industry has now paid the price.

Lawn-mower manufacturers had failed to learn the lessons painfully administered by foreign competitors to the American electronics and automotive industries, each of which had also been inwardly focused and in love with existing and traditional technologies.

In fact, the technology has now radically shifted in the lawn-mower industry – in part stimulated by the dramatic market share gains of Honda. Currently, the entire industry utilizes the blade-break and overhead valve engine technology pioneered by Honda. Everybody has it now, but Honda was first with it because they were listening to the customer and looking for a competitive advantage to better serve that customer.

Competition is all around our industries. It exerts enormous pressure on even those companies listening to their customers. It can easily destroy those who do not listen, as seen in the Honda example. Industries cannot be self-satisfied or complacent. Complacency shifts an organization's focus from its customers and its products to its personal image. It also stimulates the growth of a bloated bureaucracy which stifles creativity and initiative while promoting infighting and a 'fiefdom' mentality. These are classic trademarks of the inwardly focused organization.

Consternation

How many of us like to do work over again? Whether it's rewriting our homework, redoing a budget, or rehanging a crooked picture, rework causes all of us consternation. We would rather be doing something more productive.

'Productivity' is an increasingly popular word in the world's business vocabulary, particularly among senior management. It is one of those noble sounding yet vague and undefined terms we hide behind for fear of being asked for specifics. Invariably, 'productivity' is worker oriented and conjures up images of management forcing basically lazy, overpaid employees to work faster, harder, smarter.

Many formulae have even been developed to measure productivity, including one popular one which states:

$$\text{PRODUCTIVITY} = \frac{\text{Monetary or Unit Sales}}{\text{Number of Employees}}$$

11

Given this concept of productivity, and the general short-term nature of most management, the inevitable occurs. The workforce is reduced – whether it needs to be or not – and fewer employees are assigned more and more work. Of course, the content of their current and their additional work is never evaluated first, before this occurs. The repetitive or redundant processes are never challenged. Rather, more work processes – each with their own repetitive and redundant steps – are piled upon this smaller workforce until it is finally smothered by the mass and weight of the tasks inflicted upon it. Invariably, this all comes as a complete surprise to management.

Consternation is the by-product of this system. Consternation is caused by increasingly large numbers of employees spending more and more of their time doing work over again, because it was not done correctly by themselves, or others, the first time. Consternation occurs because inefficient, redundant, or repetitive processes were never challenged, studied, and improved.

Studies of over 40 companies in the US and internationally show that an average of one in five employees spends *all* their time doing things over again. Of course, the short-term, inwardly focused manager would just say this situation could be improved by 'firing the bastard'. Now we have four good workers!

Unfortunately, it is not quite so simple and that is why we fail to grasp the real consequences of consternation.

To increase the productivity of any organization, the emphasis must be placed on the work process, not the people involved in the process. The process must be delineated, detailed, debated, and challenged. The repetitive, redundant, 'we've always done it this way' steps in the process must be streamlined, or better, eliminated. Employees must be seen as valuable resources that cannot be wasted on rework. Thus, real productivity comes from Quality Improvement, when one in six, one in ten, then one in one hundred workers is solely involved in rework.

The goal of productivity measures is to efficiently increase the output of a work process. This is accomplished by maximizing the productive contributions of those involved in the process. Management's goal should be the development and perpetuation of a 'switched-on' participatory workforce, intimately involved with the work process and easily able to input into improving that process. Therefore, productivity would be measured not by

$$\frac{\text{Monetary or Unit Sales}}{\text{Number of Employees}}$$

but by employee initiatives or contributions aimed at improving the business process.

There is a clear precedent for this participatory measure of productivity and it comes from organizations that have realized that employee consternation is a prime ingredient to corporate failures. When companies sincerely solicit employee input and respond constructively to that input, they develop a self-fulfilling plan for Quality Improvement and the elimination of consternation.

Invariably, companies who are judged as organizations sincerely interested in Quality are those with high levels of employee involvement in the management of the organization's processes. For example, the Milliken Company of Spartanburg, South Carolina has been called America's best managed company by Tom Peters and the company also won the 1989 Malcolm Baldrige National Quality Award. Not surprisingly, Milliken management places great emphasis on direct and constant employee involvement.

The best indicator of this high level of employee involvement is the fact that Milliken averages more than 15 suggestions per year *per employee*. That's participation. That leads to productivity and the elimination of consternation.

Cost

The costs involved in business today are tremendous. This is a direct result of the increased competitive pressures we previously described. Moreover, the costs of failure are staggering. However, management invariably monitors the organization's least impactful costs in great detail and neglects, or tacitly accepts as the natural order, the major costs confronting an organization.

Specifically, the major costs incurred by an organization occur in the administrative areas, not the manufacturing locations. Yet, most cost systems focus enormous detail on every miniscule component of our manufacturing process. These same systems report, yet rarely register, the extraordinary costs incurred on a daily basis in marketing, marketing research, field sales, finance, and research and development.

In fact, it is in these areas that the greatest costs are incurred. That is why Quality is so vital for every part of an organization. The entire subject of Quality costs will be discussed in detail in Chapter Seven when we explore how to implement this system in an organization. However, two brief examples now will help clarify why costs, and particularly administrative costs, are such critical reasons for Quality and Quality Improvement.

Currently, it can take several years and millions of dollars to get a new pharmaceutical product through the American Food and Drug Administration (FDA) application process. European and Canadian regulatory agencies are equally demanding. If that product is later recalled – for whatever reason – there are enormous costs involved and much of that initial investment can be lost.

Secondly, the cost of launching new consumer products is also very high, as our markets become increasingly competitive. Additionally, the costs involved in defending existing franchises can be substantial as well, as we see in the ongoing Coke–Pepsi cola conflagration. The media budgets alone from this confrontation are estimated at a combined level of over $250 million annually [8].

The entire episode of 'New' Coke further illustrates the enormous costs facing those who 'stumble' in launching a new product. In fact, this entire launch, and the resultant relaunch of 'Classic Coke', are estimated to have cost Coca-Cola over $100 million, with $52 million spent just on advertising [9]. True, this same management did push Coke to move aggressively into other 'flanker' products – 'No Caffeine', 'Cherry Coke', 'Diet Cherry Coke'. But these ideas should have been pursued regardless, and the $100 million wasted on the 'New' Coke effort would have made a dramatic impact launching these flankers more rapidly and further holding Pepsi-Cola at bay by building upon the base business rather than launching the poorly conceived 'me-too' 'New' Coke brand.

The 'New' Coke episode also stands in stark contrast to the launch of Diet Coke which was one of the most successful new products of the 1980s because it built upon the brand's heritage, rather than abdicating it, as did 'New' Coke.

It is important to note that the costs incurred by Coca-Cola in the 'New' Coke fiasco were entirely self-imposed. These were not costs they were forced to incur because of a government edict or unfavorable legal judgement. Rather, Coke management awoke one day and realized that Pepsi had been aggressively and proactively building the Pepsi franchise. Coke had been resting on their 'patented secret formula' laurels.

Thus, 'New' Coke cannot be seen as the proactive installation of a sophisticated 'home security system' to protect a valued franchise. Rather, it represents merely the act of a misguided homeowner picking up a handgun – or in this case an assault rifle – and repeatedly shooting themselves in the foot.

Most companies cannot afford these types of self-inflicted disasters and this will become increasingly true in the 1990s as Far Eastern competition intensifies and European competition awakens. The high cost of merely competing in business today means that we must 'do things right the first time' to efficiently and economically compete.

Every time we have to do something over – whether that something is a memo, a lab report, a marketing plan, a forecast, or a product launch – we are incurring needless costs. These needless costs only serve to make us less efficient and less competitive. That can prove fatal in this era of increasing competition.

Caring

Organizations are a direct reflection of their managements. Examine any company and its employees invariably will mirror the attitudes, ideals, and even the dress of their management. IBM – monolithic, conservative, sales–service dominated, white shirt and blue suits. Apple Computers – same industry as IBM – but a different set of images. Young, fast paced, informal, non-traditional. Probably do not even own a white shirt!

Therefore, when a company's management cares, the entire organization cares. Cares about what? Cares about its customers, about serving them, about providing the goods and services they want and doing so at a fair price. Cares about its community, about those

15

living around it and their environment. Cares about its country, its competitive position in the world market, its government, and the laws it enacts.

Examine the companies that 'care' and you will find a management driven standard of conduct that permeates to all employees. The customer is treated as a valuable commodity, not an irritant. The community is seen as a valuable resource, not a disposable item to be used up, then abandoned. Our country is seen as something to respect, to support, and to safeguard, not something to gouge, to undermine, to embarrass.

Companies that 'care' understand the need for Quality because it directly impacts their customers, their communities, their country. Thus, the 'why' of Quality and Quality Improvement is usually clear, or at least easily understood once explained to organizations that care.

The same is not true of those companies and organizations that do not 'care'. The examples are far too prevalent. Exxon, Johns-Manville, Union Carbide, The Department of Housing and Urban Development, The Internal Revenue Service, most American banks, and Kraft.

Kraft. The soft, familiar voice of Ed Herlihy as the brand's radio and television spokesman. Those recipe commercials on the Perry Como Show. Kraft and the American family. Almost synonymous.

Times have changed.

Kraft ran a consumer promotion in June, 1989 in which game pieces were placed in packages of Kraft American Singles Imitation Cheese product. Consumers were to match these pieces against a separate game piece printed in local Chicago and Houston newspapers. If the game piece from their package of cheese matched that in the newspaper, they were eligible to win one of the variety of prizes. The grand prize was a 1990 Dodge Caravan LE minivan, valued at $17 000. The other prizes included Roadmaster bicycles, Leap Frog skateboards, and additional packages of Kraft American Singles. [10]

In total, Kraft budgeted the prizes for this promotion at $50 000. It probably cost them one hundred times that because they did not 'care'!

For some reason, all the game pieces placed in the American Singles packages matched the winning portion appearing in the newspaper. Kraft quickly received 10 000 'winning' entries claiming the Dodge Caravan. Just as quickly Kraft 'stonewalled'. They denied any responsibility, disclaimed any liability, and cancelled the promotion.

An important element in cancelling this promotion was the recall of all American Singles packages containing game pieces. Two days after the Free Standing Sunday Newspaper Insert containing the game piece appeared in Chicago and Houston, the Kraft field sales force had to drop everything and conduct this recall. Clearly, a sales force has more important jobs to do than wade through refrigerator cases looking for 'specially marked packages' of Kraft Singles. Yet this is a cost companies that do not care continually incur because Quality is not a priority. Moreover, the cost of this recall is rarely ever included in the total calculation of what this type of fiasco costs an organization.

While the recall proceeded, Kraft continued to deny any responsibility or liability regarding the promotion. In almost comic fashion, Kraft management shifted blame from themselves to printers, promotion companies assisting with the event, even the newspapers. Everyone but Kraft.

Yet, Kraft has an internal promotion department that coordinates these events. They have marketing departments – from brand assistants to Vice Presidents of Marketing – who are responsible for just this type of consumer promotion activity. They have an extensive legal department that must approve all such events, down to the very words used in the promotional copy, and they have Senior Management that is responsible for everything Kraft does.

That Senior Management can either unequivocally state 'the buck stops here' or they can play 'hot potato' with every difficult situation that arises.

In this instance, consumers handed Kraft a hot potato which could melt all of Kraft's cheese – imitation and natural. Because Kraft does not 'care', they were served with a 'class action suit' – certainly not Corporate America's three favorite words – by over 1000 supposed prize 'winners'. Yet Kraft continued to bluster and feign innocence. 'We think this event will end up costing us $4 million', a Kraft spokesperson stated. The legal bills alone could total that much, if not more.

Kraft would have been best served if they owned up to their problem and they could have emerged from this potential disaster as heroes by awarding all 'winners' some type of prize. However, they did not do this because they did not 'care'. They let lawyers usurp the role that senior management should play and thereby kept the customer at arm's length, instead of embracing them. What else would one expect from a company whose major contribution to Society has been Cheese Whiz and Velveeta?

Clearly, what top management does will be reflected throughout the rest of the organization, no matter what the organization.

This is best seen in Donald Regan's statement while serving as Chief of Staff to President Ronald Reagan. In trying to disavow any personal knowledge, and thus culpability, of the Iran-Contra events – and thereby place the blame on others – Donald Regan used an analogy from his days in the world of high finance. Regan – former Chairman of the Merrill, Lynch, Fenner, Pierce, and Smith brokerage house – stated, 'Does a bank president know whether a bank teller is fiddling around with the books?' [11]. Possibly not.

However, all the 'tellers' should know – and quite clearly they did in Regan's case – exactly what the 'bank president' stands for and what their and the bank's standards of conduct and 'caring' are. Quite simply, those companies and organizations that 'care' will embrace Quality and thereby stand the best chance of surviving in the extraordinary business climate at hand.

Caring companies and organizations are customer driven and understand that they have internal, as well as external, customers. These companies will maintain continuous contact with their customers, understand customers' needs and expectations, and meet – or exceed – these expectations on a regular basis. Further, these companies will understand, through Quality Improvement, that real productivity will be increased, and costs decreased, by continually improving their dealings with customers inside their organization.

For example, on average less than 20% of an organization's population actually deals with the 'end product'. However, everyone is involved in producing something within an organization – a letter, a report, an account statement, a computer printout. These are 'products' which each have internal customers, and a truly productive organization will identify these customers and serve them with the intensity and caring that it provides its external customers. That's what Quality is all about.

At first glance, it is possible that not every organization, and every individual within an organization, will be able to identify with each of these four reasons for 'making quality happen'. For instance, many organizations do not believe they have any competition. This is particularly true for departments within larger organizations or companies. They see themselves as insulated from the competitive fray, yet they too are competing – competing for budget allocations and internal funding.

For example, members of the Naval Air Force may not see any direct competition for their organization – there is not a Brand X Naval Air Force competing with them. However, this organization is certainly competing internationally with other naval air powers for readiness and superiority in flying skills. Additionally, they are competing with other military flight organizations, such as the Air Force and the Marines, for funding. Finally, the Naval Air Force – as part of the entire United States Armed Services – is in competition with a wide variety of other domestic and foreign projects for funding from the Congress. The same is just as true for the Royal Air Force and any part of any other European armed service. They are all competing with other domestic agenda items for an increasingly limited supply of funds.

The same is true for parts of our organizations. There may not be two Information Systems departments within our organization fighting it out for market share, but certainly our Information Systems organization is fighting for funding and resources with all the other parts of our organization. The decisions management continually faces are those of whether to allocate additional resources to one department at the expense of another. Therefore, competition is a very real element in any organization.

We certainly see consternation in all types of organizations. The rework, the non value-added actions that occur daily in all organizations contribute to stifle real creativity and innovation. Individuals spend increasingly larger amounts of their time doing work they

19

really were not hired to do, but that has become 'part of the job'. Therefore, they lose interest in the job, their productivity drops, and they are more susceptible to the lure of 'greener pastures'.

Consternation can occur anywhere – a teacher who finds more and more of their time involved with bureaucratic paperwork and less and less with classroom teaching, a pilot in the Armed Services who increasingly has their flight time limited due to budget cutbacks, a marketing executive who spends vast amounts of their time reworking budgets and forecasts instead of planning for future growth opportunities, the sales professional who spends all their time apologizing for non-delivery of orders or explaining incorrect billing as opposed to active selling.

Clearly, costs are everywhere in any organization. To paraphrase the rallying cry of the 1960s – 'If you're not part of the solution, you're part of the problem' – 'if you are not adding value to an organization and its products, then you are adding cost'. The best news about managing costs is that the individuals with the greatest knowledge on the subject are already in our employ – they are the people involved with each of our work processes. If we can tap into their expertise and knowledge, we can achieve incredible results in managing our costs.

Caring is the only one of the four reasons for 'making quality happen' that falls squarely into the lap of senior management. They have to look into the mirror each day and make certain they care and care passionately about their customers. There certainly are marvelous examples around us of those who do care and they have been richly rewarded by the consuming public. Sadly, there are many more who are struggling and looking everywhere for answers, when the answer lies before them in the mirror.

But Quality cannot be 'added on' in serving customers. Rather, Quality is built into an organization and its products by being competitive, by eliminating consternation, by managing costs and by caring, and this all starts at the top of an organization. Those managements and organizations that do not realize this will simply melt under the extreme pressure and heat generated by the expanding world marketplace.

REFERENCES

[1] Statistical Abstract of the United States, 1989, 109th Edition, US Department of Commerce.

[2] Scott, David L. (1988) *Wall Street Words*, Houghton-Mifflin Company, Boston, p. 24.

[3] IBID.

[4] *Advertising Age*, 26th March 1990, S-10, 28 March 1985, p. 14.

[5] *The World Almanac and Book of Facts*, Pharos Books, New York, (1989) p. 138 and (1983) pp. 125–6.

[6] 'Sit Down, Taxpayers' *Newsweek*, 4 June 1990, p. 60.

[7] Ballard, Robert D. *Exploring the Titanic*, Scholastic/Madison Press, New York, p. 11.

[8] Detroit *Free Press*, 24 July 1988, p. H1.

[9] *Wall Street Journal*, 7 March 1990, p. B1, B8; *Business Week* (Industrial Edition), 24 June 1985, p. 481.

[10] Chicago *Tribune*, 11 July 1989, p. 1.

[11] Drew, Elizabeth, 'Letter From Washington', *The New Yorker*, 29 December 1986, p. 89.

What is Quality?

2

Now that we understand 'why' Quality is important and 'why' Quality Improvement is so relevant in today's business climate, we now need to clarify 'what' is meant by 'Quality'.

In dealing with the subject of what is Quality and what is meant by Quality Improvement, there are four basic questions which should be addressed. The answers to these questions form the basic concepts of Quality Improvement. The questions, and their answers, are not difficult to understand or apply. In fact, we need only examine the standards and practices we follow in our personal lives and then apply these same standards to our business lives.

Invariably, we have two separate systems – two sets of books – one for our personal life and one for our business life. This leads to confusion, doubt, indecisiveness. We need only one standard. We can develop that standard by answering these basic questions about Quality.

What is Quality?

How do we make Quality happen?

What is our attitude toward Quality?

How do we measure Quality?

WHAT IS QUALITY?

Quality is many things to many people. The answer to the question 'What is Quality?' can be as vague and general as the answer to the question 'What is art?' 'Quality' is becoming part of the business lexicon which favors auspicious sounding yet vague words, like 'excellence', which can mean many things to many people. However, it is impossible to communicate the need for Quality or embark on a process for Quality Improvement if everyone is aiming at a different target.

Quality invariably becomes entangled with cost – quality items are seen as expensive. One immediately thinks of Rolls Royce cars, The Ritz Hotel, Rolex watches, and elegant restaurants.

Must Quality be so vague, is it purely in 'the eye of the beholder', and must it be tied to price alone? Clearly, the answer to all these questions is 'no'. A quality product or service is simply one which meets or exceeds the customer's needs or expectations. Quality is defined by the customer. It is their needs and expectations which we must meet or exceed to achieve Quality. Quality has nothing to do with cost and it is only vague and unclear when we choose to make it so.

For example, a 'quality' car is one that meets or exceeds the needs and expectations we have for that car. We are the 'customer' for that car and therefore we determine what our needs are. We may develop a list of requirements that can only be satisfied by a Rolls Royce. For example, we may be a Beverly Hills or London real estate agent selling multi-million dollar properties to Arab Sheiks. Then the Rolls would be a quality car if, in fact, it met the needs we established. However, we may have some very basic transportation requirements which could be handled by a Hyundai. If the Hyundai meets these needs, then it is a quality car.

In fact, in our personal lives we have very clear expectations for the elements most important to us. We are up at 7.00 am, want our two and one half minute soft-boiled egg, diet soda, strip steak medium rare, baked potato, martini – 'shaken, not stirred'. Specific, clear, understandable, do-able needs and expectations.

We do not go into a restaurant and 'assume' they know what we want. Nor do we tell them to bring out all the menu items so we can then sort through them, keeping what we want and discarding the rest. The chef's meat cleaver in our head would probably accompany such a request.

However, in our business life we do this all the time. We are invariably vague – 'do good work', 'our goal is excellence', 'give me a report on . . .' Our lack of specificity transfers the onus of our request to the suppliers of these various services. In fact, we are really asking them to 'read our minds'. They may, in fact, provide what we want on the first try, but that is accomplished purely by serendipity – total random chance.

Rather, we need to be specific in describing our needs and expectations. We need to spell them out in detail, obtain agreement to them from our suppliers, and then that supplier will have the information they need to 'do the job right the first time'.

Some companies have become sensitized to the need for responding to and exceeding their customer's specific needs, with excellent bottom-line results.

Consider the recent advertising for discount hotel chains in the US, such as Motel Six, Red Roof Inns, etc. Their advertising message states that the traveler may not require elaborate lobbies, elegant room furnishings, and an extensive health club if they are only using the hotel for one night's sleep as part of a business trip. The traveler's needs might be different if they were going for a week's vacation, but for a brief business trip, why pay for all the amenities which they do not use? The advertising message for these discount hotel chains emphasizes their ability to meet and often exceed the customer's needs and to do so most efficiently.

So Quality should now be defined as 'meeting or exceeding customer's needs and expectations' and these needs and expectations are determined by communicating with our customers. (Remember, we have customers inside and outside our organization, as we discussed earlier.)

Importantly, 'meeting or exceeding customer's needs and expectations' should not be confused with 'conformance to specifications'. Clearly, a product or service can be produced exactly to stated, internally agreed upon, specifications and still not meet customer needs. 'Conformance to specifications' does not necessarily mean Quality. Rather, it can be the hallmark of the inwardly focused organization which spends its resources maximizing the efficiency of its processes irregardless of whether these processes produce products customers want. A widget produced to the tightest possible tolerances is worthless if no one wants to buy it because it does not meet their needs.

'Conformance to specifications' organizations are usually dominated by manufacturing and engineering groups and tend to be highly capital intensive. Big, expensive machinery tends to dominate creative customer-oriented thinking in these organizations. The tendency is to force the organization to sell what the machines make, rather than to make what the customer really wants. This is unfortunate, yet understandable in today's cost driven business culture. Engineering and manufacturing personnel are evaluated on their efficiency and the conventional wisdom thereby dictates long manufacturing runs, few change-overs, and standardization.

However, the outwardly focused organization can maximize its market impact by directly responding to consumer needs and thereby dominate a market by serving its many sectors rather than concentrating on serving only one.

For example, the 1988 launch of Male and Female Disposable Diapers from Procter & Gamble is a classic example of the outwardly focused winning out over the inwardly focused. Procter & Gamble dominated the disposable diaper category in 1988. There appeared no immediate reason why the major investment required for the Male-Female product should be contemplated. Conventional wisdom says you have the commanding market share, your manufacturing process is clearly under control – 'if it ain't broke, don't fix it!'.

Yet, mothers have been telling market researchers since time immemorial that boys and girls have different 'wetness patterns'. This is not some recent occurrence. Nevertheless, the existing products, with some minor improvements, have traditionally been seen as 'good enough' and the substantial capital expenditure required for the necessary changes reinforced that belief. However, the Japanese have made dramatic inroads with diaper technology in the Far East and the stage was set for a repeat of the Honda lawn-mower scenario. Only this time it would occur in the $4 billion disposable diaper market, of which Procter & Gamble held over a 70% share. Thus, Procter & Gamble launched Male and Female Disposables.

Certainly, there is no guarantee at this point that the Male and Female Diapers will be a success, or that they will prevent major Japanese incursions into this vast and profitable category. However, this example does demonstrate how one manufacturer was unwilling to remain 'inwardly focused'. Rather, they dramatically changed a highly successful and capital intensive process to address customer needs.

This move also set the stage for the follow-up introduction of Procter & Gamble's 'training pants' diaper – once again a product focused on addressing a long term request from mothers with diaper age children. This type of externally focused, customer driven effort to meet and exceed mothers' needs and expectations helps Procter & Gamble maintain a commanding market share in the enormous ($4 billion plus) disposable diaper category. This strong market share translates to continued strong profit performance that can 'bankroll' further customer focused innovations on their many other products and enable them to acquire brands in product categories that complement their existing strengths.

The key to determining consumer needs and expectations is to maintain open and constant communication with our customers, whether they are located within our organization, or are the people who buy our products. We must listen to them continually, learn from them, and convince our organization that it is dependent for its very existence on serving customers needs efficiently and effectively.

This is not always the easiest road to follow, but it will be the only road to long term marketplace strength, growth, and profitability. Listening to our customers, meeting and exceeding their expectations, maintaining a position on the leading edge of the market is hard work. Short term, taking the easy way out and 'doing it the way we've always done it' may appear just as profitable and safer.

Consider the case of the young salesman who approached his District Sales Manager and complained about one very difficult account. The account was a long distance from the sales representative's home, the buyer was gruff and demanded real facts about the products presented – not merely promotional fluff. The account was only interested in what the salesman's product would do to improve inventory turnover and increase in-store traffic and profit. The account was unwilling to buy incremental volume, display, or advertise the merchandise unless the salesperson could quantitatively demonstrate real customer interest in the product.

The young salesman asked if it would not be more efficient to just skip this account – this customer – and spend the valuable sales time on some admittedly smaller, less demanding, yet potentially more receptive account.

The District Sales Manager who was not familiar with the concepts of Quality Improvement or the writings of Deming, Juran, or Crosby, responded to this doubting salesman with wisdom that is the very cornerstone of Quality Improvement. He told the sales representative that anyone can sell the 'easy accounts'. In fact, presenting to those accounts wasn't even selling, it was merely 'order taking'. 'Selling' is the active exchange of ideas, the challenging of concepts and philosophies, and the presenting of facts in an effort to produce a specific, desired behavior – the purchase of a product or the performance of a service.

Therefore, the 'real' salesperson will relish the challenge posed by the difficult accounts and will invariably succeed because lesser individuals will withdraw from the contest. Thus, those who persist not only gain the sale, they claim the 'entire playing field', and the long-term respect of their account.

The wise District Manager had thereby encapsulated the key elements of the outwardly focused, Quality conscious organization – dominate your market by meeting or exceeding your customer's needs, rather than forcing your customer to accept your requirements. By meeting or exceeding your customer's expectations, particularly the difficult or challenging ones – the ones you could use as a reason to drop the customer – you further differentiate yourself from your competitors. In reality, you are placing another 'brick in the wall' that separates you from your competition and thereby further secures your hold on your marketplace.

Meeting and exceeding customer's needs and expectations are critical priorities in the ISO 9000 International Quality Standards and in the criteria of the American National Quality Award, the Malcolm Baldrige Award. The ISO 9000 standards place specific emphasis on the need for customer review of product and service needs and expectations and the Baldrige criteria are equally demanding on the entire subject area of customer 'requirements' determination. Therefore, we are on very solid ground when we focus on our customers and plan on meeting and exceeding their needs and expectations.

HOW DO WE MAKE QUALITY HAPPEN?

The traditional view of Quality is that it is expensive and labor intensive. 'We can get you all the Quality you want – and can afford – if you just get us more inspectors!' This view holds that you achieve Quality by sorting the good from the bad – the traditional Quality control concept.

Quality control is seen by the organization as those people who suddenly appear, take the product of our process, and perform some magical test upon this product to determine if it is 'good enough'. 'Good enough' for what and for whom? Good enough for the customer or our internal, inwardly focused, standards? And do the needs of these two groups match? This view of Quality reinforces the belief that Quality is 'someone else's job' and this makes Quality achieved through inspection and appraisal very expensive.

Invariably, inspecting Quality into a product or service is far more expensive than building Quality into that same service or product. Inspection is based upon the belief – or more likely, the hope and prayer – that we can somehow 'catch' the 'bad' ones before they get out, or possibly we can rework them in the field. Many companies even advertise their 'service departments'. The real function of these groups is merely to rework the defective material that we did not catch before it left our shipping dock.

Consider how we 'make quality happen' in our personal lives. We fasten our seat belts in our cars, we make sure we have our booster shots, we brush and floss our teeth, we try to eat correctly and get sufficient exercise. We practice prevention. Consider the alternative in each case. Which would you prefer?

Therefore, we need to apply this same system to our business lives. We need to practice prevention at work. We need to take the time upfront to make certain that systems and processes work as they are supposed to, not merely wait until after they have broken down. We need to take the time upfront to establish clear needs and expectations with our customers so that we can provide the goods and services they want and provide them 'right the first time'. That's prevention.

The key to prevention is a proactive management style. This type of management is always seeking to serve their customer 'better, faster, smarter' and more completely meet their customer's needs. The alternative is the reactive management – continually firefighting and implementing short-term 'quick fixes'. Invariably, their justification for this style is that 'we don't have time now' to overhaul a problematic process – 'we have to stay in business!'

Miraculously, we never seem to have the time up front for adequate planning, yet we always have plenty of time to do it over again once it's gone wrong! This time for rework usually appears on weekends, after 5 pm each afternoon, and in place of our vacations!

In fact, the proactive organization takes the time upfront, understands their process, maps out how the process will move from inception to completion – the process 'flow' – and challenges itself by asking, upfront, 'what could go wrong?' This is the key question.

Who should be asked? Those directly and intimately involved with the process. Talk with your organization. Get their insight into potential problems before they become problems. The people doing the work – whether in accounts payable, commercial production, market research, or on the factory floor – have the best insight on what can go wrong with a process and how it can be improved.

In place of communicating within our own organization, we often choose to employ expensive outside consultants. In fact, a good measure of how reactive or proactive a company is can be determined by how much that organization spends on outside consultants dealing with existing technology and problems. The inwardly focused, 'quick fix' mentality is very willing to 'buy' solutions, thus they invest heavily in outside consultants.

And what do these consultants do? Almost without exception, their first step is to interview the people in our organization – exactly what we as managers should be doing. Then they summarize their findings and regurgitate them back to us, their client. The classic middleman, consultants merely tell us what our people told them. They then package it nicely and charge exorbitant amounts. Of course, the truly classic reactive organizations – those completely out of touch with the concept of prevention – will not only employ these costly consultants, but they then derive perverse pleasure in completely disregarding the recommendations they have paid so dearly for!

The international ISO 9000 Standards focus on this recommended proactive approach through an emphasis throughout the standards on clear process definition, documentation, and auditing. Similarly, the Malcolm Baldrige National Quality Award criteria stress a proactive approach by a continuous emphasis on process improvement based upon customer needs and expectations.

Quite simply, the era of the reactive management style is over. Not everyone has gotten the message, but it is only a matter of time. The companies who will succeed in the 1990s will be those committed to long-term growth, prevention, and a very special attitude towards Quality.

WHAT IS OUR ATTITUDE ABOUT QUALITY?

The inspection process for achieving Quality normally includes the stated, or unstated but clearly implied, standard that some mistakes or nonperformance regarding customers' expectations will occur. This is seen as acceptable, if regrettable. After all, it is a complicated world, we are only human, nobody's perfect, etc. At least we can budget and plan for them.

Consider applying that logic to your personal life! Do we tolerate incorrect paychecks, inaccurate bank balances, improper credit card billings, imprecise medical treatment? Clearly, each of these is a very complicated process with enormous opportunities for error, but do we blithely accept that mistakes will happen to us and accept them? Probably not. In fact, we are – or certainly should be – infuriated when these type of occurrences take place.

What is our attitude about Quality when we travel by plane, when we consider the interstate transportation of nuclear wastes, when we contemplate the possibility of ground water contamination? Is some level of error acceptable? Do we want to be on the receiving end of that 'some margin of error'? Probably not.

Therefore, we need to apply that same attitude toward Quality to our personal and business lives. This is an attitude of continuous

31

improvement. Simply, this means that we will not tolerate mistakes, and if they occur, we will seek to eliminate their causes forever and continuously improve the processes producing our goods and services.

Continuous improvement does not mean perfection. 'Perfection' is a term for poets and philosophers, not pragmatic professionals. In a business context, 'perfection' is another vague, indefinable word, as 'Quality' once was. No one is asking anyone to be perfect. Rather, we are asking everyone to develop clear expectations for their processes by communicating with the customer(s) of their process and then meeting – and possibly exceeding – those needs and expectations the first time, every time.

Importantly, continuous improvement encompasses the vital communications link with our customer. What is it they want from us? How can we better serve them? Remember, a customer is not a bother, but the basis for our business. The better able we are to meet their needs and expectations, the better opportunity we have for building our business.

Therefore, continuous improvement is the desire to continually improve the goods or services we provide to our customers. Continuous improvement is a vital component to long term Quality Improvement.

We have discussed some examples of continuous improvement in our personal lives, but what about in business? Where has this attitude been applied?

In 1976, a young marketing manager doing some field sales training in Portland, Oregon decided to take advantage of a very attractive sale at a major Portland department store. SONY televisions were being clearance priced at $464.00 for the 17″ screen model. The department store sales personnel explained that these were closeout models because SONY was eliminating the rotary channel dial on these models for a new, push button format.

The sale was made and the young marketing manager bought his first color television – a SONY no less. After money changed hands, the sales clerk informed the purchaser that the SONY was an excellent television and that he was to be congratulated on buying the largest screen that SONY was able to produce. 'The 17″ screen is the limit of the Trinitron technology, they can't build a bigger screen.'

However, if in the future the marketing manager would like to buy a bigger screen television, he should come back and see some larger screen sets from Magnavox, RCA, and Zenith. Some 'with the works in a drawer' – an unusual product feature we will discuss more fully later!

So the 17″ television screen was the extent of SONY Trinitron technology in 1976. This was the Maginot Line between SONY and the US television industry. Screens of 17″ were the DMZ, the 38th parallel, the line in the sand. 'This is it, you ain't comin' any further!' You can almost hear John Wayne intone these words, smell the six-gun holster leather, and feel the prairie dust burn your nostrils!

Next time you visit a major sports stadium, take a moment to examine the ubiquitous big screen televisions used in the scoreboards for replays, coming attractions and even commercials.

All produced by great American companies – SONY, Mitsubishi, Sharp!

So what happened? How did SONY move beyond the 17″ screen? Wasn't that the 'limit' of their technology? In fact, it probably was the limit – in the first six months of 1976! But SONY did not see that technological boundary as a permanent barrier. Instead, they pressed ever forward! How?

By having an attitude of continuous improvement. The Japanese call this *Kaizen*. SONY saw the 17″ screen barrier as a temporary hurdle, rather than as an end. They continually challenged themselves, their technology, their thinking.

Isn't it remarkable that America is a nation forged by pioneers of primarily European extraction who overcame extraordinary challenges, yet so many of our current industries have taken a 'stand pat' attitude toward the challenges of technology, innovation, and Quality? Fly over the Rocky Mountains in the American West, look at their stark and desolate beauty, and then consider the character of the people who fought their way westward over, around and through these behemoths. If our predecessors crossing the plains and facing the challenge of the Rockies had possessed the timid attitude seen in the majority of current American management, the Los Angeles Dodgers and San Francisco Giants baseball teams would today be playing baseball in Omaha, Nebraska and Topeka, Kansas and the Rockies would be the Pillars of Hercules – the end of the known world!

Continuous improvement: never satisfied with the status quo. Knowing full well that what works today may be obsolete tomorrow. This prospect could terrify managements continually looking for the next 'home run' or 'hole in one' in their business. In fact, what is actually needed is a series of singles or deftly placed approach shots. Too often we look toward the major breakthrough, the blockbuster new technology or product formulation. Rather, we should strive for the hundred small changes which in the end dramatically improve our product or process and keep us well ahead of our competition.

Masaaki Imai, author of *Kaizen – The Key to Japan's Competitive Success*, states 'Successful companies have shown that it is possible to anticipate change and to meet the challenges while they are still manageable'. These organizations are able to effectively anticipate changes in customer's needs and expectations because they focus on their customers and are in constant contact with them. Constant customer contact means 'no surprises'.

Continuous improvement also puts to rest the great business canard that the first one to market with a new process or product will reap the greatest rewards. In fact, myriad examples exist of companies that innovated and then 'rested on their laurels', content with having created a new category or business.

In every case, these companies were quickly and dramatically superseded by companies offering further improvements that more completely addressed customers' needs.

In the SONY television set example, we referenced the Magnavox 'works in a drawer' televisions. These television sets were developed and aggressively marketed based upon their 'works in a drawer' construction. This design allowed for easy access to the television set's tubes and interior circuits when repair or replacement was necessary. The clear – though unstated – implication was that these television sets would malfunction at some time and would require service. However, that service would be easy to perform because 'the works' were in an easy to access drawer in the set's front panel.

Quite probably, this design represented fairly sophisticated and advanced design – among television sets depending on tubes. This technology represented the industry paradigm at the time. Yet this television paradigm is exactly analogous to the many other industry paradigms that have limited management's long term, customer driven focus. (Joel A. Barker addresses the traps of paradigms and provides other excellent and thought provoking examples – such as the Swiss Watch Industry's paradigm concerning the quartz watch – in his book *Future Edge*.)

Just as in the case of the Honda lawn-mower, SONY was not content with building a better 'works in a drawer' television. They were not first in the television marketplace. Instead, they challenged the industry paradigm and won in sales, market share, profits, and customer satisfaction by focusing on better meeting customer needs and expectations.

Other examples where first into the market did not guarantee long term success are plentiful. Consider the birth control pill – launched by Searle – now dominated by Ortho Pharmaceuticals, with Searle a market nonentity. Or acetaminophen, which has replaced aspirin as the pain reliever of choice in most countries around the world. First introduced by Bristol-Myers, the market is now dominated by the Tylenol family of products from McNeil Consumer Products. Previously, we discussed disposable diapers, but who today realizes that Chicopee, Incorporated invented and marketed the first disposable diaper? Procter & Gamble now controls close to 70% of this $4 billion category and Pampers is almost synonymous with disposable diapers around the world.

The examples go on and on. First to market is no guarantee of success. First with what the consumer wants means success, growth, and profit. That's continuous improvement!

Both the Baldrige National Quality Award criteria and the ISO Standards emphasize the need for continuous improvement. In fact, the Baldrige criteria emphasize that for all major processes within an organization, there should be a clearly defined process for improving them on an ongoing basis. While the ISO 9000 Standards are less specific, they clearly recognize the need for continuous improvement by the very fact that recertification under the standards is required. Therefore, even organizations that have received the coveted ISO 9000 certification cannot assume that they 'are set for life'. Continuous improvement must be their way of life!

35

So how will we know when we are becoming more Quality conscious? How can we see if prevention is becoming a way of life in our day to day business operation? How will we know if continuous improvement is a universal attitude at our organization? Simply put, 'How do we measure Quality?'

HOW DO WE MEASURE QUALITY?

The traditional inspection view of Quality incorporated the belief that Quality was not only to be 'inspected in', but that it was also the realm of experts who could differentiate the 'good' from the 'bad': the 'I know it when I see it' or 'wine tasting' school of Quality. This viewpoint certainly saw Quality as unmeasurable. How do we measure a feeling we have about something?

Clearly, if we define Quality as 'meeting or exceeding customer's needs and expectations', then we can measure when, and how often, we are not meeting those needs. By clarifying the definition of Quality, we have also clarified how we measure it.

Moreover, by measuring when we do not meet our customer's needs, we can attribute costs to these instances. Therefore, our measurement of Quality can become consistent with the language of all important business measurement – money. We measure sales, inventories, profits, return on investment, back orders, accounts receivable and payable. All are measured in money. Now we can measure Quality in 'the coin of the realm' as well.

How? We can measure this cost of non-Quality by simply calculating what the incidents cost us in time and material. Did we have to rework some item or report? How much time did that take? Did we have to scrap some material? What was the cost of that material and how much time was involved in scrapping it? It is really quite simple, yet deadly accurate in portraying an organization's Quality status.

Many are uncomfortable with this direct approach to measuring Quality. However, the measurement of Quality is only vague when we want it to be. Moreover, the measurement of Quality must incorporate the entire organization, not just the manufacturing area which traditionally suffers the most intense 'Quality' scrutiny.

Actually, an organization's major non-Quality costs are administrative and management related. Relatively speaking, an organization's smallest non-Quality costs are incurred in the manufacturing area because they have been under such heavy cost scrutiny for so long. Administrative/management costs are often mistakenly considered the 'cost of doing business'. It is all too often a very high and unnecessary price to pay for a real lack of management discipline.

Consider the fact that over 40 separate companies in the US, UK, Canada, Europe, and Asia, varying in size from $10 million to $500 million in sales, have determined that their cost of non-Quality averages over 20% of gross sales. Moreover, the majority of these costs are incurred in the administrative/management areas, not manufacturing.

Examples? Here are two.

One of the most expensive parts of consumer goods marketing is the development and production of television advertising. In the development stage, the 'client' may require the involvement of assistant product directors, product directors, group product directors, and marketing vice presidents. The advertising agency can be represented by two or three levels of account management and an equal number from the creative and art direction departments during the same development stage.

In the actual commercial production stage, this cast of characters can increase fourfold. Therefore, it is imperative that companies have a clearly defined commercial production process and clearly communicate this process to their advertising agencies and their own personnel. Some companies do. Many do not. Here is what happened to one that did not.

A meeting is usually scheduled before the actual filming of television commercials in order to review all factors involved with the upcoming production. As a 30-second television commercial can conservatively cost $150 000 to produce, these meetings can be incredibly valuable if expectations are agreed upon and consistently met.

These 'pre-production' meetings will usually review the final commercial script and determine that it has been approved by client management, client and agency legal departments, and the television networks. (Surprisingly, the people who brought us *Dynasty*,

Dallas, and *Geraldo* would not allow a toilet bowl to be shown in commercials for many years. A significant hurdle if you happen to be marketing a bowl cleaner!)

Additionally, a 'shooting board' may be part of the review. This board details how every frame of the commercial will be filmed. Wardrobe and the actual shooting location, or studio setup, are also covered. Finally, the actors and actresses – the talent – are interviewed.

Many companies have a clearly stated policy that all talent with speaking roles in commercials must be present, in person, at these pre-production meetings. This enables client and agency managements to see exactly what these people look and sound like today. A minor point? Hardly.

At one pre-production meeting, the advertising agency covered all the agenda items and then presented eight by ten inch glossy photographs of the recommended talent. Every actor and actress has a set of glossies – usually called head sheets – which may contain a series of facial angles or poses. Many are heavily retouched, some quite outdated. None present the performer exactly as they will look on film or video. This can only be done by seeing the talent 'live'.

In our example, agency management informed the client that the 'talent' was unable to attend the pre-production meeting because they were at another shoot. Instead, the agency presented the eight by tens and some 'recent' Polaroids. (Many clients also have a clearly stated requirement that not only will the talent be present at the pre-production meeting, but they will also not be on-air in any other commercials concurrent with the planned production. With 95% of actors and actresses out of work, why give all the work to the currently employed 5%?)

Client management, except for the newly appointed product director, had departed the meeting by this juncture, leaving the junior product director surrounded by agency management, creatives, and art directors – all with years 'in the business'. The product director hesitated, not liking the looks of the proffered photographs. 'She looks like the "Bride of Frankenstein", haven't we got someone else?'

The agency, whose commission is based upon the production and airing of advertising, closed ranks. 'We'll fix all that with makeup.

38

She had her hair cut since these pictures. Trust us, she's great. Everyone wants her. We're lucky to get her!' (Again, remind yourself – as all client management should – that 95% of all actors and actresses are starving and willing to work at 'scale'. How come most agencies can only find the busy ones, the ones who charge us 'scale and a half' or 'double scale' and require special hair and makeup support people? Remind yourself as well how an advertising agency makes its money!)

The next day, at the actual commercial set, the product director finally came face to face with the talent. She still looked like the 'Bride of Frankenstein', even in person. When this concern was presented to the agency, the product director was assured, 'We can fix that with lighting, some makeup, camera angles, and soft focus. Trust us'. The product director was unsure, 'What if you can't, shouldn't we just get someone else?'

The advertising agency management then 'dropped the hammer'. Surrounded by over 40 technicians, film crew members, makeup artists, grips, sound people, and caterers, the agency Management Supervisor stated flatly, 'Are you authorized to scrap to-day's shoot? We already have a "sunk cost" here of at least $10 000. Are you willing to eat that? Do you have the authority to?'

Confronted by this senior agency manager – the counterpart of her boss' boss, the vice president of marketing – the product director demurred. She would 'trust them'. Maybe it would come out right in the editing stage. Maybe they could shoot the commercial through a 'Doris Day' filter and the talent would look more like 'Rhoda' and less like 'Rhodan'.

The commercial was completed, finished produced, readied for airing, and then scrapped upon final review by the client. Never to see the light of day. The talent still looked like the 'Bride of Frankenstein' in the finished commercial!

$150 000 scrapped. The 'cost of doing business'? Hardly!

A clear cost of non-Quality. There was an established process – or should have been. It had a customer – the company paying for the commercial. The process and the client who developed the process had clear expectations – 'live talent at all preproduction meetings' – and that expectation was not met. The cost, $150 000. Totally avoidable.

Or consider the case of the major firm that was determined to increase sales on its third largest product. This product was continually overshadowed by the company's two larger brands, so management decided that what was needed to remedy this situation was an elaborate selling piece presenting the product's great benefits and features. A great sales brochure would certainly spur this brand to new growth!

Management disregarded the fact that the brand was significantly premium priced to its closest competitor, yet performed only at parity. Moreover, management neglected to consider that annual advertising had been halted half way through each of the recent years in order to maintain the brand's dollar profit level which continued to erode as the price premium to competition increased and unit volume dropped. An elaborate sales brochure was the answer to all these problems – consistent with the old advertising adage, 'When you have nothing new to say, sing it!'

So work began on the brochure. In fact the word 'brochure' does not do justice to the item. It was a hard bound, three ring notebook which opened into a desktop presentation. The pages featured four-color artwork and graphics. Additionally, it included color product photographs, sample print advertisements, and even several die-cut pages which could be opened and closed to reveal additional product attributes and benefits. This elaborate production then fit into a hard bound slip cover, suitable for placement on the most distinguished and exclusive library shelf. Now this was a selling piece!

Each of the 150 field sales representatives received a copy. Of course, by producing only 150 copies, all printing economies of scale – the more you print the cheaper the per piece price – were eliminated. The total cost for development and production – $50 000.

Half way through the brochure's development a new product director assumed responsibility for the brand. The sales brochure project was already under full sail, with complete management support, so the 'new kid' devoted time to larger issues – like increasing unit sales volume.

As part of the learning process on the new business, the product director decided to spend time in the field with the sales force. It was felt this would provide important insight into accounts' and customers' reactions to the product and develop improved rapport between marketing and sales.

Despite these good intentions, Home Office Sales Management gave very specific requirements about how product directors should comport themselves while traveling with sales representatives – 'don't talk about their cars, they'll complain they're too small', 'don't interfere with the actual sales calls', 'speak only if spoken to while visiting accounts', and 'try not to get in the way'. Clearly, a lot of work was needed in the area of improving marketing and sales rapport.

While on the road, the product director, hoping to catch sight of the recently distributed sales piece, would surreptitiously peek around the car's interior. Sometimes, when they stopped for gas or lunch, the product director would search through the car looking for the brochure. No sight of it anywhere!

On subsequent trips to the field, the product director started to see what appeared to be pieces of the sales brochure in various hand-done personalized sales presentations created by the individual sales reps. These presentations were usually cardboard sheets with colored market graphics which sales reps might use to present 'profitunities to Bill's Big-Buy'. Occasionally, a product photo or business trend graph from the $50 000 sales brochure would show up in these presentations.

Exasperated, and seeing no evidence of any use of the full brochure, the product director threw rapport to the wind and confronted his sales host, 'Did you receive that elaborate brochure we sent you on ''Brand X''? Where is it and how come I never see you or any other sales reps using it? Do you know that it cost us $50 000 to produce that thing?'

The somewhat astonished sales rep responded and explained that, no, the sales force was not using that brochure. In fact, most accounts did not like mass produced, 'generic' sales presentations 'from headquarters'. Rather, they preferred a customized approach which directly addressed how a specific product, or sales promotion, would impact their market, their customers, their in-store traffic, their profits.

General brand selling pieces which did not address these individual account issues were basically useless. Sales reps kept them in their garages or used them to insulate their attics, particularly in the northern latitudes.

As you begin to faint, you first lose your peripheral vision. Everything starts to appear as if you are looking through one of those cardboard cores at the center of a roll of paper towels. The room becomes very hot, your muscles assume the consistency of gelatin. Then you lose consciousness.

Some $50 000, and who knows how many development hours of editing, rewriting, approving, and resubmitting, and they're sitting in someone's garage next to the cat litter. Or maybe being used as cat litter!

After reviving the product director, the sales rep tried to clarify the situation. 'We never asked for those books – too heavy, too awkward, and accounts hate "home office" stuff! Nobody ever asked us what *we* needed!'

Steadying himself against the sales rep's car door, the product director ventured, 'Well, what do you need to help you sell "Brand X"?'

'Color package cuts.'

Again, the faint sequence begins and the product director begins sliding down the side of the car toward the onrushing asphalt.

'Color package cuts' are sheets of adhesive backed product pictures, usually in color. There may be 20 small color pictures of the product on each sheet – very much like children's stickers. These color package cuts are used to augment presentations or letters. In quantity, they probably cost less than five cents a sheet.

'$50 000 and all you needed was color package cuts? I think I'm going to throw-up!'

The rest of the trip was very quiet, but from then on that product director always asked what people wanted before developing any sales materials. The $50 000 cost of non-quality was a heavy tuition, but the lesson was learned, at least by one person.

These examples are not anomalies. They are not the work of stupid, ill-intentioned, or untrained people. Importantly, they are just as important and costly whether they impact internal or external customers. Examples like these surround every activity in all industries. They are happening in your organization as you read this.

Far too often we have assumed that these events were part of the 'woodwork'. We now know they are not 'the cost of doing business', we now know they should not be tolerated, and we now know they can be measured, translated into a monetary value, and thereby provide us with an excellent indicator as to how we are progressing with Quality Improvement.

By measuring Quality in financial terms through the cost of non-Quality, management can not only learn what is really happening within their organization, but they can also become more efficient and effective. They can do this by now concentrating their efforts on the real problems confronting the organization. These real problems are identified through the cost of non-Quality as those items having a significantly negative impact on earnings.

Therefore, management can concentrate their efforts on these 'significant few' items that directly impact their external and internal customers and disregard the 'trivial many' upon which they had previously lavished far too much valuable time. This is consistent with the Deming approach which led to the initial Quality revolution in Japan and which is detailed in *Dr Deming, The American Who Taught The Japanese About Quality* by Rafael Aguayo.

Now that we have answered these four basic questions about Quality – 'What is it?'; 'How do we make Quality happen?'; 'What should our attitude toward Quality be?'; and 'How do we measure Quality?' – the answers form the basic concepts of Quality:

- Quality is defined as meeting or exceeding customer needs and expectations – requiring that our organization be customer focused;
- we make Quality happen through prevention – requiring the adoption of a proactive management style;
- our attitude toward Quality must be one of continuous improvement – requiring the constant challenging of processes and paradigms;
- Quality is measured by the cost of non-Quality – requiring the effective use of data and information concerning our failures to meet customer expectations.

What do these concepts do for our Quality Improvement efforts? They provide a clearer picture about what is meant by Quality, but

43

how do we now apply them to begin Quality Improvement? We have now addressed the 'what' of 'What is Quality?', but that leads to another, related question. Now that we have these four basic concepts of Quality, what do they do for us? How do they help us initiate Quality Improvement?

The four basic concepts of Quality define the nature of our Quality Improvement effort. This effort is characterized by these four basic concepts and what they represent – a common language, a proactive management style, an attitude change, and a long-term orientation towards our business.

COMMON LANGUAGE

The four basic concepts of Quality provide a common language that everyone, at all levels of our organization, can understand. Additionally, if our organization is multi-regional, or multi-national, we have a common way of communicating about Quality. It will no longer be an imprecise or vague subject. Whether we are in Bangor, Maine or Bangkok, Thailand, when the term 'Quality' is used, we will now know that it means 'meeting or exceeding customer needs and expectations'.

Building this common language is a vital step in improving our communications, both internally to our organization and externally to our customers and suppliers. In fact, most organizations find that their major problems are communication based. Invariably, we all believe we are great communicators, thus we devote little or no time to refining this skill and therefore, what skill we may possess diminishes or completely disappears.

Poll any group of managers, from any discipline within an organization in any industry for their number one problem, and at last 90% will volunteer communication related problems. An important step in addressing this problem is a common language of Quality. Now we have one.

PROACTIVE MANAGEMENT STYLE

A recent television commercial for a major bank shows a business executive bemoaning the lack of 'creative problem solvers' within his organization. All too often business management relies extensively on crisis managers and fire fighters. These are people who can come into a troubled situation or organization, clean it up, and then 'ride off into the sunset' to fight more fires another day. The business press is continually extolling the virtues of such characters without ever reviewing or revisiting their long-term impact on an organization.

Unfortunately, the successful fire fighter in business is all too often more fiction than fact. Their solutions are usually short-term fixes – flashy 'grandstand' plays which rarely address the real root cause of the original problems. The 'fire fighters' ride off in glory and leave the organization with the smoldering embers of a problem that one day will explode again into the original problem. However, the conventional wisdom states that 'we'll wait till that happens, then react'.

Instead, our new commitment to prevention as the way we cause Quality requires that we adopt a proactive approach. Therefore, our troubled business executive should be searching for a proactive problem preventer. Our goal is to prevent problems and to accomplish this by being proactive. This involves advance planning and forethought. It means challenging accepted ways of doing things, accepted practices, paradigms, and the 'conventional wisdom' of 'we've always done it this way'. It means focusing on meeting or exceeding our customer's needs and expectations.

Remember that they had always done it 'this way' at American lawn-mower manufacturers and this attitude allowed Honda entry into their market. And there was plenty of 'conventional wisdom' and ingrained habits in the American electronics and automotive industries as well, and this reactive management style almost invited the proactive and customer focused Japanese to devour major segments of these markets.

A proactive management style asks 'what do our customers really want and need' and 'what could go wrong?', not 'what went wrong?' To move from one style to the other will also require an attitude adjustment.

ATTITUDE CHANGE

Management must adopt a new attitude towards the conduct of business. The first part of this attitude is that they will lead – really

45

lead – the company on its journey to Quality Improvement. The second part of this attitude change must demonstrate management's commitment to customer focused continuous improvement.

We can no longer accept as inevitable that certain problems will occur in our operations. We must find out the cause of these problems and eliminate them forever. Further, we must continually seek to improve our work processes so that they most efficiently and effectively serve our customers – we must be a management that sincerely 'cares' for our customers. We'll never exceed their needs if we fail to sincerely care about them.

For some, this type of attitude change may seem dramatic, even drastic. Others may be there already. It is important to realize that Quality Improvement will not happen overnight. We did not get into the situation we are currently in as either a country or a company overnight, and we will not get out of it that quickly either. It will take time, but now is the time to begin and our new attitude must convey that sense of urgency.

The attitude of Quality Improvement is really identical to that in our personal lives, as we discussed earlier. If we have one standard of Quality, one attitude for Quality Improvement, and it is consistent in both our personal and business lives, then our journey to Quality Improvement is less arduous and will be more easily accomplished.

LONG-TERM ORIENTATION

In the past few years, it has been exceptionally popular, even faddish, to become interested in the 'Japanese Management' style. Executives jet to Japan for extended visits to a variety of Japanese industries. They usually return to their American organizations brimming with ideas like 'Just In Time' (Kan-Ban) [1], 'Continuous Improvement' (*Kaizen*), the need for raw fish in the company cafeteria and noon time exercise classes. They also want it all implemented *yesterday* and they delegate this implementation.

They have completely missed both the message and the secret of Japan's success and Europe and America's chance to regain their worldwide industrial status.

46

Japan's success has been directly attributable to both their long-term view of the world marketplace and their customer focus. They wisely realized that they could achieve a position of major commercial impact over time if they really studied their customers and their customers' needs, if they persisted and continuously improved their products and services targeted at these needs, and then improved the processes by which these products and services were produced. The Japanese were not impeded by the classical European and American financial horizons – 'if it doesn't pay out in 12 months, forget it!' Rather, the Japanese were willing to invest in new equipment, new technology for the longer term payback.

It may not make short-term financial sense to scrap fully depreciated machinery which is still producing effectively in order to phase-in new technology. 'Our output may suffer short-term, we'll have to train people on the new technology, and we're not sure it will really pay out in the required time period.'

However, it also does not make any kind of financial sense to one day wake up with an entirely obsolete technology – fully depreciated or not – and your competition running away with the market. Just ask the American steel industry, ask Detroit about their one-time commitment to drum brakes while disc brakes were being introduced by European and Japanese car makers. Ask the people trying to compete with Procter & Gamble in the capital intensive diaper business but who were unwilling to make the required technology and capital investments to meet and exceed customer needs and expectations.

The Japanese have a saying that even the largest rock will one day be broken down by a continuous dripping of water. It may not happen today, it may not happen tomorrow. It may not happen in our lifetime, but it will happen. It is inevitable.

The same is true for Quality Improvement if it is as constant as that drop of water and if we are as constant in our resolve and possess a long-term, customer focused horizon.

REFERENCE

[1] The 'Kan-Ban and 'Just In Time' concepts are detailed in Shigeo Shingo's book, *The Toyota Production System*.

How?

3

We have now seen the many reasons 'why' Quality is such a vital issue for business today and 'why' Quality Improvement needs to be at the top of management's agenda. And now that we have clarified 'what' is really meant by Quality and 'what' benefits it will provide our organization, we can concentrate on 'how' we go about 'making Quality happen'.

Our overall goal in implementing Quality Improvement is to make Quality an integral part of our organization's culture. It should not appear to be some extra appendage or stand out like a poorly planned home addition orchestrated by mad King Ludwig. Rather, it should be part of the accepted and expected conduct of our business.

We will accomplish our goal of a customized Quality process by tailoring it to our specific organization. It is vital that the process be *our* process, that we control and direct it, not vice versa. The Quality Improvement process is a means to an end – the end is Quality as an integral component of our organization's practices and 'persona'.

We must never lose sight of that fact and let the process itself become the driving force. This can happen if the process is too bureaucratic, too static, too inflexible.

There is no one way, nor one right way to implement Quality Improvement. The process presented here has been successfully implemented at major organizations in a variety of industries. Each tailored the process as required by their location, workforce, and corporate culture.

This is not a 'how-to' approach for obtaining ISO 9000 certification or for winning the Malcolm Baldrige National Quality Award.

However, the approach in this book is complementary to both these important Quality Improvement milestones. This book emphasizes the establishment of a customer-focused strategic Quality approach that is critical to the foundation of the ISO 9000 process and that is a *sine qua non* for the Baldrige criteria. Without the customer-focused foundation that is the basis of this approach, neither ISO 9000 certification nor even consideration of the Baldrige criteria are realistic or practical.

Importantly, the Quality Improvement process presented in this book is designed specifically *not* to promote bureaucracy, nor does it require additional headcount or fulltime administrators. Certainly, elements such as additional bureaucratic layers or incremental personnel would be counterproductive to our entire goal of a more efficient and effective organization. If a Quality Improvement effort ever becomes bogged down in bureaucracy, if the process takes precedence over the long-term organizational goal, if the effort becomes counterproductive or counterintuitive, then it is time to step back, review, reassess, and possibly reread this and subsequent chapters.

IMPLEMENTATION APPROACH

Each element of the recommended Quality Improvement process presented will be addressed through our three basic Quality Implementation questions – why, what, how? These three questions will address the specifics of the recommended implementation actions. They will address the objective of each recommended action, the strategy for accomplishing that objective, and the tactics required to execute our strategy. In this mannner, we will develop a simple, yet thorough implementation plan for Making Quality Happen in our organization.

GETTING STARTED

Where to begin? Start at the top!

Any effort to change an organization, its culture, and its management style must start 'at the top'. This means that the people who run the organization must be 'on-board' before any implementation begins. It is not necessary that they all totally comprehend every nuance of the Quality Improvement process, but they must be clear about the organization's overall direction concerning Quality and be committed to Quality Improvement as a goal for their part of the organization.

INITIAL QUALITY ORIENTATION

The best way to begin this implementation process is through an orientation on Quality. The objective of our initial orientation on Quality with top management is to solidify our overall direction concerning Quality and obtain management's commitment to making it happen in their part of the organization. This orientation should be attended by the management team. In our example we will refer to this group as the 'management board'. This group comprises the line managers and the management of the staff functions supporting the organization.

Many times one overall topic can be used as the focus for the orientation. 'Quality' is probably too abstract a subject at this juncture within our organization, so the discussion could start by examining market-share trends, customer service levels, inventory levels, product recalls, customer satisfaction research results, scrap levels, or expedited freight expenditures. Any of these general business topics will quickly lead into a discussion of Quality.

Orientation participants should be asked for their views concerning the cause of the topic 'problem'. Going around the room, we will probably find numerous causes and we will probably also see the defense mechanisms of the various business units begin to surface. This desire for self-preservation and a 'fiefdom' mentality are integral parts of the corporate culture we are trying to change. Invariably, no clear reason why will be established for the specified problem, but participants may start to see that they are not really working in an orchestrated fashion with one another and that communication within the organization appears to be less than ideal.

51

We can now move the discussion from one specific, predetermined topic to a topic chosen by each participant. Specifically, each participant should now be asked for their leading 'Quality' problem. A more specific introductory direction should not be provided, as it will be important organizational learning to determine just what each participant views as a 'Quality' problem.

These individual problems should be listed on an easel for ready reference. Further, it is very important that all participants understand what each item means when it is presented. Specifically, one participant may say their leading Quality problem is vendors. This participant should then be asked to clarify and expand upon that – what about vendors is the problem? Is it their lack of timely delivery, the fact that products are not consistently produced to specifications, inaccurate billing, etc.?

With this detailed list of Quality problems completed, we will be able to see several key items which reinforce the need for a Quality Improvement process. First, the participants each presented a Quality problem and probably did so without a great deal of prompting or reflection. Therefore, we have clearly established a 'need' for Quality Improvement and this need is a vital prerequisite in obtaining agreement for implementing a Quality Improvement process from this management board.

Secondly, the Quality problems listed by the participants will invariably be internally focused. They will all be items we have done to ourselves, rather than problems caused by competitors or outside forces. Additionally, they will only rarely be customer focused and supported by quantitative data or facts.

Finally, the problems will almost universally be communications related – people not talking with each other, departments not talking to each other, lack of clearly established needs and expectations, little or no specific management direction, and assumed procedures which sometimes are followed, but which most often are disregarded or circumvented and thus become counterproductive.

The key learning from this exercise is that we have Quality problems, we cause them, and we must do something about them, because no one else will or can!

We have now covered the 'why' of Quality Improvement in this orientation. Therefore, we must provide the solution to the problems identified by the group and that is the 'what' of Quality Improvement. This can be addressed through a clear and concise presentation to the management board on the four basic concepts of quality.

In presenting these concepts to the group for the first time, it is important to emphasize how the concepts tie to our personal life standards and practices. This makes them clearer, more realistic, and more palatable. Additionally, we can refer to the problems outlined on the easel by fellow board members and discuss how establishing clear customer needs, prevention, continuous improvement, and 'the cost of non-Quality' address these issues. By doing so, we begin to become more comfortable with these concepts.

In most cases, the problems we have outlined reflect a lack of clearly understanding customer needs and this can be emphasized as we present and discuss this concept. Further, organizations usually have extensive problems caused by the lack of preventative planning and proactive thinking. Again, the concept of prevention can be reinforced as we cover the problems cause by its absence.

Continuous improvement is easily juxtaposed to situations where managements have become enamored with one way of doing things, our internal paradigms – whether it is manufacturing ('we always have high scrap rates, we're very demanding!'), marketing ('we only buy Prime Time Television, we don't like Cable Television or Radio!'), or even customer service ('you have to expect some complaints, after all everybody makes mistakes!').

Finally, assigning a monetary value to our problems will really add impact to their breadth and scope. A useful exercise for the orientation would be to roughly estimate the cost of non-Quality for the problems listed on the easel. Even the crudest of calculations will show that these costs are significant, unnecessary, and thereby rob the organization of vital financial and personnel resources.

ORIENTATION SUMMARY

At this point, the Management Board should be 'sold' on the need ('why') for Quality and on the basic concepts ('what') that will form the basis of our Quality Improvement effort. What may be unclear is 'how' the organization will now proceed to address these issues and that is the next topic on our agenda. However, it is important to assess the overall tenor of the management board before detailing implementation steps for Quality Improvement. We will require a firm foundation of management commitment and ownership of Quality upon which to build our Quality Improvement process and we should take the time now to assess the strength and depth of that foundation.

People who have achieved the management board level are usually independent thinkers, knowledgeable about their specific discipline, and skeptical about the ability of outside forces to improve their business situation. They have invariably achieved their stature in the organization by making things happen and getting results. Therefore, some skepticism about 'how' Quality Improvement will address their specific disciplines is natural and should be anticipated. After all, to openly admit that they had problems, and that they cannot solve these problems themselves, would be counterintuitive to the very nature of most management board members.

So, some skepticism should be anticipated concerning the 'how' of Quality Improvement. In addressing this skepticism, it is vital that the entire subject of Quality and Quality Improvement be presented as a positive step at improving our competitive position, not as a remedial exercise necessary because of shortcomings with this management group.

CHANGING A CULTURE

Through our Quality Improvement efforts, our emphasis must be on addressing and improving processes rather than correcting and disciplining people. The corporate culture we are trying to change is one in which people are always held accountable for problems, mistakes, and failures. Yet, organizations spend enormous amounts of time, effort, and resources hiring the brightest, most capable individuals. We then terrorize them into mediocrity and risk-aversion by emphasizing people rather than processes when problems arise.

Almost all employees sincerely want to do their best, to contribute in a positive way. Yet, often these best desires are frustrated and

54

impeded by procedural problems and this is where Quality Improvement will focus its efforts. We must not be an organization that mirrors that classic and climactic scene in the movie *Casablanca* where Vichy French Police Chief Louis orders the gendarmes to 'round up the usual suspects' in order to protect Mister Rick who has just shot the evil Nazi Major Strasser. We must not be an organization that 'rounds up the usual suspects' when problems occur and we must set that tone in this management board orientation, lest fear of reprisal block the group's receptivity.

Therefore, we need to carefully determine where each board member stands on the subject of Quality and Quality Improvement. Their entire organizations will quickly mirror their level of support, so a candid discussion on the subject is vital at this juncture. The sceptics should be encouraged to raise questions and express their concerns. Many times initially sceptical board members become zealots for Quality and Quality Improvement once their concerns surface and are addressed.

Those who remain unconvinced, or even antagonistic – whether it is outwardly displayed or not – may need to discuss their problems and concerns in private with the management board Chairperson. It is critical that these issues surface early, to let those concerned vent their fears, doubts or questions.

Most concerns or questions relate to a lack of specific knowledge about the process of Quality Improvement, and that is natural. We have not even addressed the specifics of Quality Improvement at this time. We are merely trying to achieve consensus on the 'why' and 'what' of Quality. The 'how' will be tailored to our needs and expectations.

Often, this will calm the fears of those concerned that some program is going to be jammed down their throats by outside consultants. Sadly, this type of experience has been all too prevalent in industry. Accordingly, organizations and their managers are always dubious about new 'miracle cures' and the new 'flavor of the month' when it comes to business panaceas.

THE QUALITY RENEGADE

Those who remain intransigent after such clarification – and this represents very, very few individuals in our experience – must decide their future course. If Quality is really important to an organization, and if the time and effort required to successfully implement an effective Quality Improvement effort are being marshalled, then everyone must do their part.

A successful Quality Improvement effort will require cooperation, commitment, and ownership by all management personnel. A crew team isn't going to win any regattas with only seven of the eight rowing, nor can a relay team win consistently with three runners going full out while one cruises. Further, organizations may debate how safety programs are implemented, but they do not allow some parts of the organization to disregard safety procedures, nor do they tolerate partial compliance. And so it must be with Quality and Quality Improvement.

In fact, we really have to question the thought process of individuals who would be concerned about, or troubled by, the prospect of an organization that communicates effectively – both internally and externally – an organization that practices prevention and plans long-term, and an organization that continually tries to improve all aspects of its operation. Possibly, we are better off without such individuals.

Quality Improvement cannot be left to 'bubble up' within the organization as some top level sceptics will advise. Such individuals will mask their scepticism through delegating the process to lower levels within the organization. Many times sceptical management will even cooperate in visible Quality events – they will read the speeches you write for them, stand in the right place, and smile at the appropriate time, but without understanding the words or believing them in their hearts.

Quite honestly, none of the so-called 'world-class' companies – defined as those who have won the Malcolm Baldrige National Quality Award or Japan's Deming Prize – have ever done so with a management team that delegated Quality. Nor is it possible to obtain ISO 9000 certification with a management team that does not own Quality and the organization's Quality Improvement effort.

Invariably, the opposite is true. These world-class managements have delegated everything but Quality which they have relentlessly owned, championed, driven, and lead. And because organizations are a direct reflection of their senior management, these organizations have Quality as an integral part of their culture – from the top down! For them, Quality is a way of life – inseparable from their day to day operating mode.

INTRODUCE QUALITY IMPLEMENTATION ACTIONS

To conclude this initial orientation on Quality, the 'how' of Quality Improvement should be introduced. It is not necessary to cover these implementation actions in detail. That will be the subject of a later planning session. However, organizations – and particularly management boards – are action oriented, so some discussion of 'how' Quality Improvement will be implemented is appropriate.

The seven implementation actions for Quality Improvement in any organization are:

1. management ownership of Quality and Quality Improvement;
2. Quality implementation team in the form of the management board;
3. Quality training for the entire organization, to understand the 'why' and 'what' of Quality and 'how' everyone is involved;
4. measurement and the use of the cost of non-Quality to prioritize problems for solution;
5. corrective action to eliminate the identified problems forever;
6. a quality council to provide internal market research on the progress of the Quality Improvement effort;
7. awareness and recognition programs to inform the organization about Quality and reinforce our implementation actions.

This brief introduction on the seven elements for implementing Quality Improvement is really all that is necessary at this time. It would be overkill to use this initial session to also plan a complete implementation schedule for the process. The initial orientation can be concluded with a sign-up sheet on which board members can sign up for leadership of one of these seven actions.

Actually, the management board Chairperson will be responsible for both channelling management ownership and directing the Quality implementation team. Therefore, the remaining five elements can be divided up among other board members. (Co-chairs are always appropriate if there are more board members than actions.)

It is very important that each management board member has a stake in the implementation. No one should be allowed to 'sit this one out'. The more sceptical or uncommitted should be paired with the zealots because their enthusiasm is often contagious.

A follow-up implementation session should be scheduled at the conclusion of this initial orientation. It should follow closely – no more than two weeks later – to maintain the momentum and 'top of mind' position. The objective of the upcoming implementation session is to detail the components of each Implementation Action and develop a total implementation plan for our Quality Improvement effort.

In the upcoming chapters, each of the seven Quality Improvement implementation actions will be examined in detail, providing a step by step guide to winning the Quality revolution. This is exactly the type of detail that should result from our organization's planning meeting on implementing Quality Improvement.

Each implementation action will be examined through our three basic questions – 'why is the action necessary?', 'what does the action entail?', and 'how do we implement this action?' These questions form the outline of our objective, strategy, and tactics for each implementation action.

Clearly, there is no one right way or one magic formula for implementing Quality Improvement. However, the format presented here can serve as a framework or starting point for our own customizing.

Implementation action 1 Management ownership of Quality and Quality Improvement

4

The first action required for implementing Quality Improvement is communicating to our organization management's ownership both of Quality and the Quality Improvement process. Therefore, the objective of this implementation action is 'to make it perfectly clear' that the organization's management is dedicated to Quality, committed to Quality Improvement, and fully responsible for the planning, implementation and success of our Quality Improvement efforts. This message must be absolutely clear to the entire organization and it must be continually reinforced through actions, not just words.

Clearly, if an organization is going to implement the type of cultural change required for successful Quality Improvement, this will only be accomplished with our line management leading the parade. The organization knows full well that management will drive what it believes is vital for the business. Currently, this includes quarterly profits, market share, return on assets, etc. Management never delegates its role in directing these vital measures, and so that's 'why' they must also lead on Quality and clearly communicate to the entire organization their ownership of and commitment to Quality.

Many times the terms 'commitment' and 'involvement' are used interchangeably when discussing 'what' is meant by this initial action of 'management ownership and commitment'. However, there are important differences between the two words and a simple analogy should clarify them. Commitment and involvement are like ham and eggs. In ham and eggs, the pig is committed, the hen is involved. Therefore, we want our management committed, not merely involved. We want them to own the process, as we own our home – we are concerned about our investment and want to make certain that investment grows and prospers.

In demonstrating this commitment and ownership, management's actions must be synchronized with its words. Remember, to an organization, perception is reality and all organizations are far more intelligent and perceptive than they are ever given credit for. If management 'talks a good game' and reinforces that talk with visible actions, the organization will quickly realize the depth and reality of management's commitment and ownership. The organization will then adopt this commitment and become co-owners of Quality and our Quality Improvement efforts.

In our discussion of management ownership of Quality and Quality Improvement, we will use the term 'management board' to represent that group of line and staff managers who direct the daily operation of our organization.

This management board can take a variety of forms. In an operating company it probably will be the senior management team comprising those reporting to the company's President or Managing Director. In a local school board, it would be the school board president and the other board members. The captain of the aircraft carrier *USS Theodore Roosevelt* and his wardroom – the ship's senior officers – act as the ship's management board. In a variety of non-profit organizations the Executive Director and their staff make up this leadership team for Quality Improvement.

The key point to remember is that whoever has final responsibility for the successful operation of an organization must have the responsibility for, the commitment to, and the ownership of Quality Improvement.

MAKING MANAGEMENT OWNERSHIP VISIBLE

'How' this visible display of commitment and ownership is accomplished is straightforward. First, the entire management board should present the organization's Quality Improvement plan to the employees. It is important for employees to hear these goals and implementation plans from the mouths of their management. Preferably, this communication should be done in a 'live' and interactive situation.

Next, management must look for visible ways of reinforcing this verbal commitment. Possibly, this can involve taking actions to dramatic lengths to prove a point. What matters most is that the message is clearly communicated. That is what we want.

For example, one organization had developed a culture in which meetings never started on time. Never. People could wander in 10 or 15 minutes after published start times and still feel certain that the meeting would not have started. At the other end, meetings never had any scheduled 'end times'. They merely ended when the highest ranking person in the room ran out of things to say.

As usual, there was always a great deal of organizational moaning about too many meetings, meetings running late into the evening, and meetings never starting on time. Yet, no one did anything to remedy this situation because management was the major culprit. Therefore it became an accepted part of company culture – 'it's always been this way'.

When the organization's management became involved in Quality Improvement, they immediately seized on this meetings issue as a way of galvanizing and publicizing their commitment. They agreed that they would get to meetings before the publicized starting times and then make certain the meeting began on time – no matter who was, or was not, in the room.

The organization's president had the first opportunity to implement this plan when he addressed a strategic planning meeting. He arrived five minutes before the start of the meeting. First he mingled with the other early arrivals and conducted the small talk before the meeting began that can take up the first half hour of most meetings. He then closed and locked the meeting room door at one minute after the meeting's scheduled start time. Late comers tugged at the locked door, in vain. After approximately ten minutes of cooling their heels, they were let in, without any word or rebuke, but with the meeting clearly in progress. They sheepishly crept to their places.

The president closed the session by announcing the date, location, and start time of the next meeting. In detailing the start time, he added just a little extra emphasis to the words 'promptly at 9.00 am'. That message went through the organization as if the building had been hit by lightning. Within minutes of the meeting's conclusion everyone in the entire building – and possibly the entire staff at distant locations as well – knew what happened and who had been left outside, madly tugging at the locked conference room door.

Meetings began to start on time. Agendas started to be published before meetings were held. Soon agendas even carried times for each agenda-item and end times began to appear as well. No one stood around with a stop watch to clock these entries, but a heightened awareness of the value of employees' time had been raised. The Quality Improvement process had begun and begun with management clearly acting as its owners.

Another important way of demonstrating management commitment and Quality's priority to the organization is to include Quality Improvement in the personnel evaluation criteria of our employees. The expression 'what gets measured gets done' is never more true than when our boss sits down and reviews our objectives at the start and end of a period and Quality Improvement is on that scorecard.

Clearly, it is important that these objectives be specific, measurable, and realistic. Examples of such objectives include that managers will attend the first wave of Quality training, that they will review the training with their direct reports, that corrective action teams are formed from within their area, that customer-focused measurement charts are up to date and visible. These are just some items which can easily be made part of a manager's annual performance evaluation.

In conclusion, management ownership of Quality and Quality Improvement involves a 'watch my feet, not my lips' management style. Actions, not words, are of paramount importance. The organization needs to be made aware of these actions – and we will cover how to do that when we discuss awareness and recognition. But management can spread the word through 'managing by walking around'. Tom Peters extolled the benefits of this management style in his landmark Quality book, *In Search of Excellence*. Everyone talks about the benefits of managing this way, yet it rarely gets done. Management complains that it is time consuming. Yet, what should be consuming more of management's time than understanding exactly what is happening within our organization, particularly as it regards our customers.

For example, generals can receive all the staff briefings possible. They can pour over aerial photographs of the battle front until cross-eyed, but they will receive the clearest picture of what is transpiring by visiting the trenches and talking with the frontline troops. This way they can clearly evaluate the situation and the spirit of their fighting force – the people who are being called upon to 'make it happen'.

The same is exactly true in business, yet most managers spend their time safely ensconced in their offices at headquarters, shut off from the real work of both the organization and our customers.

A widely circulated story in Quality Improvement has a young Toyota Motor Company executive returning from receiving his MBA training in the US and immediately trying to implement his US training upon returning to Japan. The recent MBA reproaches the chairman for his propensity to wear the uniform of the assembly-line workers, as this does not reflect the chairman's exulted role in the organization. Additionally, the MBA recommends that the chairman spend more time in his office where he would be more accessible to visiting chief executives and journalists looking to learn the secrets of Toyota's success.

When the chairman was asked why he spent so little time in his office and so much time with the auto assembly workers, he replied, 'I don't spend my time in my office because we don't build any cars there!'

Whether the story is apocryphal or not is irrelevant. It clearly demonstrates at least a perceived level of management commitment to Quality Improvement at Toyota and perception is, after all, reality. Just as clearly, it is a story whose main characters could not be substituted for any of Detroit's 'Big Three' management and still be believable. Therein lies the dilemma when it comes to management ownership of Quality Improvement.

Both the ISO 9000 standards and the Malcolm Baldrige criteria are particularly adamant concerning the leadership role senior management must play in Quality Improvement. Moreover, both are exceptionally clear that responsibility lies with the 'highest level of management' in the wording of ISO 9000. The Baldrige criteria go even further to detail exactly who this highest level entails. The goal of both the Baldrige criteria and ISO 9000 is to avoid the shifting of responsibility for Quality to that amorphous 'them' that we often refer to when we seek to shirk responsibility or ownership.

Quality and Quality Improvement will only be successful if the men and women responsible for the direction of our organizations own and are also committed to and responsible for Quality. They must clearly communicate this ownership both in their words and actions because Quality will have a real and direct bearing on our organization's future direction. Their ownership can make that future either bright with success or its absence will cloud it with failure.

IMPLEMENTATION ACTION 1: SUMMARY

Let's summarize this first implementation action and highlight some specific actions to take.

1. Communicate management's ownership and commitment to Quality and Quality Improvement with the entire organization as quickly as possible once we have decided to actively pursue Quality. Strive for face-to-face communication with the organization so immediate feedback and questions and answers are possible.
2. Develop a 'road show' for management to take to distant locations, if we have them, or to our sales force. Do not let these important groups be 'out of sight, out of mind'.
3. Look for 'quick wins' to demonstrate management ownership and commitment in a real and tangible way. For example, take a firm stand on product or service deviations. Focus the organization on its external customers by having employees meet with customers or attend customer focus group discussions. Bring customers to our location and set up a regular schedule of management board visits to our key customers. Dramatize the need to become customer driven and focused on our customers. Start meetings on time. Publicly recognize others who have

demonstrated real ownership of and commitment to Quality and Quality Improvement.

4. Manage by 'walking around'. Budget some time each day to look, listen, and learn what is happening around the organization. Arrange meetings with key customers to clearly understand their requirements. Make these meetings a regular part of the work process, not an exception.

5. Reinforce our ownership of Quality Improvement to our organization by assisting them in complying with customers' needs and expectations through providing the resources required for making Quality happen.

Implementation action 2 Quality implementation team | 5

The Quality implementation team directs and oversees the implementation of a Quality Improvement process within an organization. It is universally true that the success of this team is directly proportional to their level within the organization. Any organization sincerely interested in Quality Improvement will make their management board their Quality implementation team. This group of managers is responsible for the direction of every activity of any substance within the organization and therefore they must lead and direct our Quality Improvement effort.

If the implementation is delegated, the organization will clearly see this as a signal of Quality's lower priority and who within an organization is going to spend time on low priority projects?

At world class organizations such as Toyota, Federal Express, Milliken, Xerox, Nordstrom's and Motorola there is no question as to where Quality and its customer driven focus reside among the organization's priorities. The organization is clearly and uniquely focused. This makes their task that much easier, for there is no need to decipher the 'management tea leaves' or to learn about 'this week's priorities'. World class organizations are crystal clear on their customer focused priorities and thus can spend their time more productively satisfying their customers and thereby building their market shares and profits.

The objective of the Quality implementation team is to plan and implement the Quality Improvement effort. This is accomplished by assigning one of the Quality implementation actions to each management board member. They are responsible for developing an organization-wide implementation plan for this action. Clearly, the purpose of this book is to significantly simplify the development of that implementation effort. However, each board member must tailor their Quality Improvement action to the entire organization. Their leadership role within the organization and their knowledge of its operation will help them accomplish this.

Of course, it is certainly appropriate for board members to recruit others to assist them in developing their implementation plans. A small team (five to six members) of action oriented individuals from a variety of business disciplines will greatly facilitate tailoring the process to our organization.

IMPLEMENTATION TEAM MEMBER RESPONSIBILITIES

As members of the Quality implementation team, each board member is actually responsible for two activities. First, they are responsible for their specific Quality implementation activity – such as the development of a corrective action system; organizing an awareness and recognition process; or planning the education of all employees and suppliers. Secondly, they are responsible for the total implementation of Quality Improvement within their area of line responsibility. Therefore, the Vice President of research and development may be responsible for developing a measurement and cost of Quality system for the entire organization. He or she will develop this system and recommend it to the Quality implementation team for organization-wide deployment.

Further, this individual is also responsible for the implementation of Quality Improvement within the Research and Development organization, for example. No one else is going to be making Quality happen within their organization unless they do. Quality Improvement cannot be 'topically applied'. Rather, it must develop systemically, from within organizations. Nothing will get less attention faster than any 'program' that an organization feels is being foisted upon them from unknowing sources outside their area.

MULTIPLE LOCATION ORGANIZATIONS

Organizations with multiple locations must adapt their Quality implementation team to their organization. For example, our organization may have its headquarters in London. We also have manufacturing sites in Texas and Puerto Rico and international offices in Chicago and Budapest. There should be a headquarters' Quality implementation team in London and additional teams in Texas, Chicago, Budapest, and Puerto Rico.

The headquarters' team should consist of the organization's management board and should develop the overall organization-wide plan for implementing Quality Improvement. This plan would certainly include implementation schedules for all locations. These schedules should be developed with input from the management of all locations.

The Texas, Chicago, Budapest, and Puerto Rico facilities should each have their own Quality implementation teams. These consist of the management of that facility – the manager and their immediate staff, for example. This group would be totally responsible for implementing Quality Improvement at their facility. They should work closely with the headquarters' team in order to tailor the plans developed at headquarters to their locality.

In developing an overall implementation plan, the Quality implementation team should take the time upfront – prevention – to examine organizations in their geographic area that are already involved in Quality Improvement. It is not necessary that these organizations be in the same industry. What is important is that our organization begin to look outside its own walls and begin learning from others. There is never a need to 'reinvent the wheel'. Rather this is the time to ask that great question, 'if you had to do it over again, what would you do differently?'

It would also be profitable to visit those organizations that are viewed as having 'world class' Quality Improvement efforts. Many of these organizations have been described in detail in the business press and are invariably very interested in sharing their experience with others. Companies at this world class level realize that there is nothing proprietary about Quality Improvement and they welcome the opportunity to share, so we should benefit from their experiences and tailor them to our organization. This type of Quality Improvement process 'benchmarking' is an increasingly popular means of eliminating and avoiding implementation problems in your organization. Through this type of benchmarking we can learn from others and profit from their experiences. (The subject of Bench-marking is discussed in greater detail in Chapter Seven.)

A favorite question to ask during these sessions – regarding any implementation issue – is 'if you had to do it all over again, what would you do differently?' The response to this question may not fit our situation exactly, but we should certainly listen and be receptive to those who have 'blazed the implementation trail'.

INTERNAL IMPLEMENTATION TEAMS

Structurally, it is not necessary for each division within an organiza-tion to have its own Quality implementation team. For example, in research and development there is no need for a Quality implemen-tation team unique to research and development. Rather, the manage-ment of that organization should be responsible for implementing Quality Improvement as an integral part of their daily job. Therefore, the traditional management team in research and development will form the Quality implementation team for that function. A key element of this implementation will be to guarantee that the plan developed by the organization's overall Quality implementation team is executed as planned in this division.

The entire implementation goal is to avoid duplication of effort and to concentrate on the organizational benefits of a Quality Improvement effort rather than to become bureaucratic. The head-quarters team plans and oversees the entire implementation. The location teams tailor the plans developed at headquarters to their unique situations. It is that simple. We will address the headquarters and location implications of each Quality improvement action as it is addressed in its respective chapter.

QUALITY IMPLEMENTATION OPPORTUNITY

The start of a Quality Improvement effort provides an organization, and particularly its top management, with an unique opportunity to re-examine its *raison d'être*. Specifically, many organizations

70

plow along year in, year out without ever really stepping back and examining either where they are, or worse, where they are going or want to go. We all get lost in the day to day work and thereby lose sight of what our 'work' should really accomplish. Most often, organizations become internally focused, concentrating on what the organizational bureaucracy needs to sustain itself as an entity. They fail to focus on what the organization's customers require or need from us so that we can remain a viable entity in the market place.

A clear example of this internal focus are the procedures and policies generated by the internal bureaucracy. These policies almost always relate to the needs of that bureaucracy and do not in any way focus on the needs of the customer, internal or external. These policies are all around us. These internally focused policies have probably become part of our 'organizational woodwork' – we probably do not even recognize that they exist. These ingrained and internally focused procedures are like the costs we incur for failing to meet our customer's needs or expectations – we just assume that they will always be with us.

For example, senior management may decide that our inventory levels are too high and unilaterally order them reduced, in the absence of any real plan or process to do so. Significant customer inconvenience results when orders go unfilled, but management is pleased because inventories are down. We won the inventory battle but lost the war for customer satisfaction and loyalty.

Or consider our health benefits process – if our organization can still afford one! It may make us ask who it really benefits. In many organizations, insurance benefit forms are complicated and the benefits payment process slow and disputes rampant. However, instead of correcting this problematic process, those overseeing it focus their attention on critiquing benefit submissions and those submitting them. Employees lose valuable work time with seemingly endless form re-writes, but the benefits bureaucracy is 'just following orders' and will keep doing so until our organization finally grinds to a halt.

Or what about our frontline employees who directly represent our organization to our customers? Many organizations undermine these critical employees with needless policies and procedures aimed at serving the internal bureaucracy rather than our customers. Often, these frontline employees are unable to address customer inquiries, requests, or concerns without first clearing their actions with 'headquarters' and usually doing so in triplicate.

An example of an internally focused procedure of no value to our customer is the customer call report or sale report often required on a daily basis of field sales personnel. Dutifully prepared, they are sent to headquarters where they only gather dust, yet they are produced every day, year in, year out. The real purpose of our field personnel is to effectively represent our organization to our customers and build our sales volume, yet we waste their valuable time with useless report formats because 'we've always done it that way'. This only diminishes the morale of these key employees and this low morale is easily perceived by our customers.

World class organizations know that customer satisfaction starts with satisfied employees. This is a lesson our Quality implementation team must remember because their actions directly impact the organization in a significant way.

We have the opportunity at the start of our Quality Improvement effort to clearly re-evaluate our organizational objectives and refocus on our customers. An important first step in this process, and one that should be lead by the Quality implementation team, is the determination of our organization's 'critical success factors'. These factors are those processes which we must execute flawlessly and continually seek to improve if our organization is to remain viable. They represent the true core of our organization, the basic 'blocking and tackling' without which we will certainly fail, and sooner rather than later.

Critical success factors differ with each organization, but here are some examples developed by a wide variety of different groups.

A nuclear aircraft carrier wardroom determined that its critical success factors included:

1. the need to operate efficiently and effectively in a multi-service – Navy, Army, Marines, Air Force – environment, such as that experienced during 'Operation Desert Storm' and 'Operation Provide Comfort';
2. the need to maintain full operational readiness and capabilities with less personnel, material, and funding;

3. the ability to serve as a self-sufficient platform for both offensive and defensive military operations as well as for life support efforts such as 'Operation Provide Comfort' for the Kurds in the aftermath of the Persian Gulf War;
4. the need to maximize creative input from all levels of the ship's crew, regardless of rank or area of expertise, in order to increase operating efficiency in a budgetary environment which may see the military's funding cut by one-quarter.

An operating company developed a slightly different list of critical success factors, but they are interestingly focused on maximizing employee involvement in generating key process improvements. This organization developed three basic critical success factors:

1. the need to better understand their customer's needs and expectations and to measure the organization's performance regarding these needs and requirements from the customer's vantage point, particularly as compared to their competitors;
2. the necessity of dramatically improving new product launch cycle time with a target of halving the previous cycle time;
3. the establishment of a process for soliciting and capturing employee ideas concerning both specific process improvements and new product ideas.

A non-profit professional association that found its membership dwindling and its administrative costs rising developed strikingly consistent success factors:

1. the need to factually determine the needs and expectations of its membership rather than assuming what this rapidly changing membership body needed;
2. an increase in effective internal communications between association departments to better serve the membership and to represent the association to the membership with a common voice, not one which varied depending upon which department members contacted;
3. the need to dramatically increase association employee participation in improving service levels to the membership and in achieving increased operational efficiencies without sacrificing member satisfaction.

These critical success factors really become the focus of each organization's strategic plan. Often, the strategic planning process is an empty charade which organizations annually conduct because 'we've always done it that way'. The actual operation of the organization bears little resemblance to what has been extensively and exhaustively developed and detailed in the strategic plan. This exercise represents just another internally focused process of no value to our customer and clearly perceived by the organization as fruitless and a classic waste of their time by an uncaring management.

In contrast, our critical success factors provide a viable focus for our organization and establish clear and measurable goals towards which we can channel our efforts, and those of the entire organization. Our Quality Improvement effort will be a key strategic weapon in achieving these critical success factors. It is vital to remember that Quality Improvement is strategic in nature. It is not an end in itself, but rather *how* our organization will achieve its customer-focused objectives as detailed in its critical success factors. So the very first task the Quality implementation team should tackle, after it has formalized its internal structure, is to focus on developing the critical success factors for their organization.

While the Baldrige criteria and ISO 9000 do not refer to the role of a Quality implementation team specifically, they both mention the need for a Quality policy and Quality objectives that are defined and developed by the most senior management in the organization. The Baldrige criteria go one step further in asking how an organization knows that its employees understand and have adopted the principles covered in the Quality policy. To successfully address this item, an organization has to objectively demonstrate that its employees understand and practice the tenets of the organization's policy. This will only occur if our management owns our Quality effort and is directly in charge of its implementation through their role on the Quality implementation team.

IMPLEMENTATION ACTION 2: SUMMARY

Let's summarize the key actions for developing a Quality implementation team:

1. The Quality implementation team should comprise the organization's management. If an organization has a headquarter's location and multiple sites, then each should have their own Quality implementation team.

2. The headquarters team, comprising the management board of the entire organization, should develop the overall implementation plan for our organization. This plan can include an implementation schedule for our other locations, but need not contain detailed implementation plans for each location. This plan should be developed based upon learning gained from other successful Quality Improvement organizations.

3. Location Quality implementation teams will 'tailor' the master implementation plan to their specific location. Their objective should be to 'tailor', not 'reinvent the wheel'.

4. Board members should be assigned responsibility for the planning and implementation of at least one of the Quality implementation actions. They may form a team to assist them, although this is not always necessary.

5. Board members are also totally responsible for the implementation of Quality Improvement within their discipline.

6. The Quality implementation team should develop a short list of critical success factors for the organization. These represent the processes at which we must succeed in order to survive as a business entity. These success factors should be externally focused on our customers, not internally on serving our bureaucracy. These factors will become both the focus of our organization's strategic plan and our Quality Improvement effort. They should be quantifiable and measurable.

7. The Quality implementation team should frequently review the status of the implementation efforts in all locations to determine progress, problems and potential for new learning which could be shared with the entire organization.

Implementation action 3
Quality training

6

None of the Quality implementation actions will have more broadscale impact or be more important to the entire organization than Quality training. The objective of Quality training is to make our entire organization, and every person in it, functionally literate on Quality and Quality Improvement. Strategically, we will accomplish this by conducting training that provides the organization with a common objective, vision and language of Quality.

It is frankly impossible to broadly implement Quality Improvement until the entire organization has a common understanding of what is meant by Quality. Until that is accomplished, any widely implemented efforts run the risk of leading the organization off into a variety of different directions, consistent with the various views Management has about what is, or isn't, Quality. Thus, it is a necessity to have a common understanding and language of Quality at the outset.

All world class organizations possess this unified voice concerning Quality and their organization's critical success factors. Organizations such as Toyota, Milliken, Xerox, Federal Express, Philip's and Nordstrom's all send one message to their employees. Invariably this message focuses Quality Improvement efforts on the critical success factor of satisfying customers to the point of delighting them by dramatically exceeding their needs and expectations.

To achieve this objective, Quality training should be a broad brush stroke tailored to our entire organization, not customized by function, department, or division. Again our goal is to unite the organization under the umbrella of our Critical Success Factors and Quality

Improvement. Therefore, the Quality training effort should be a shared one organizationally.

One Fortune 100 organization formed a new company by combining two smaller operating units with related customer bases. This new organization used the opportunity provided by its Quality training process to introduce its critical success factors to the new organization. These critical success factors included the need to focus on customer satisfaction through increased internal teamwork and employee involvement.

The Quality training materials focused Quality Improvement efforts on these key organizational objectives and provided a unique opportunity for developing a unified vision, culture, and approach from the organization's inception. Again, the Quality Improvement effort was correctly seen in this instance as a strategic direction for achieving the organization's customer focused objectives.

Additionally, in our Quality training we want to promote the concept of a continuously improving organization – one that is always pushing the state of the art, not trailing far behind. Interestingly, while many professions place great emphasis on continuing education – some even requiring a specified number of training hours per year for practitioners – most businesses take an almost disparaging view of training.

The same is not true of either world class international or American organizations. For example, employees at several world class companies receive an average of 40 hours training per year. In Sweden, the government subsidizes business training. This results in close to 25% of the workforce in training at any one time. Conversely, one Fortune 100 company recently discovered that its managers averaged two weeks of training in an average *career*. Is it any wonder that the 'state of the art' is rarely originating in the US?

Our goal is *not* to have an organization that is continually in training. This is impractical and unrealistic. However, we do want an organization that is always *learning* and has a bias for knowledge and new ideas. We want to promote the concept of an organization hungry for knowledge and improvement. One that is open to new ideas, concepts, and techniques. We want an organization that seeks to learn more about its customers in order to serve them more efficiently and effectively. An effectively conducted

78

Quality training process will set the stage for future learning as a natural part of our work rather than as an infrequent novelty.

ORGANIZING QUALITY TRAINING

Importantly, Quality training must start at the top, with our management board. Even though they have been through the previously discussed orientations, and even though they have formulated the overall Quality implementation plan, they must still participate in training with the rest of the organization. Preferably, they will be trained with fellow employees from throughout the organization. In some organizations – Xerox for example – top management actually conducted the training for the next management level. This is a true 'trickle down' approach to training and left no questions concerning management commitment or ownership.

This 'top down' approach is consistent with our clear position that an organization reflects the views and actions of its management. Few opportunities for demonstrating management commitment and ownership are as effective as management's sharing the Quality training experience with employees.

Many times situations will arise that may make this management board training difficult, or at least inconvenient. Again, this is the perfect opportunity to reinforce management commitment and ownership. One organization that began implementing Quality Improvement decided that the management board would be trained separately, as part of their regular board meetings. Further, only one of the organization's Quality trainers would be allowed to conduct the training. What type of message did this send to the entire organization? How can we consider opening the environment of our organization for honest improvement when the management does not even want to share in the training of its own employees?

So make the Quality training classes 'top down' and mixed with employees from several levels. Importantly, the mix should not be so broad that lower level employees feel threatened or awed by management personnel in their training sessions. This is certainly an issue which varies by organization.

Some training sessions have been very successful including management, secretarial, and even line production employees because the organization already possessed an open environment. Employees knew their management and they were not concerned about speaking out. Management even started some of these sessions by admitting problems and difficulties. Other organizations, less open, have experienced little or no participation from lower level employees in training sessions where management was present.

As a general guideline, the classes should be mixed by organizational levels which are in normal contact as part of day-to-day operations. Further, it is very important to mix the sessions functionally. Specifically, get representatives from finance, marketing, operations, research and development, and other functions in all sessions.

There are two fundamental reasons for doing this. First, it builds organizational unity by increasing contact between these groups through the shared experience of Quality training. Invariably, one of the biggest causes of intramural friction within an organization stems from the fact that functional groups don't mix. They work separately, lunch separately, socialize separately. This prompts an 'us versus them' or 'bunker' mentality which is unhealthy and completely contrary to the unifying goals of Quality Improvement.

The second benefit of a functionally mixed class is that it enables employees to see that we all share common problems. Invariably, each functional area, and in fact each organization, believes their problems are unique. Quite the contrary, most problems are common no matter what the industry, organization size, or functional area. And most of the problems relate to our inability as individuals and organizations to effectively communicate with one another and with our customers.

SHARED TRAINING BUILDS TEAMWORK

Additionally, most of our problems are caused by our own internal processes and actions, not by external forces. This is a great awakening for many and very beneficial when it occurs in a functionally mixed environment. The 'good news' is we can usually quickly address the internally generated problems.

We can further build the strength of our new organization by promoting the team building aspect of our training through in-class team projects, presentations and peer recognition. We have found distinct improvement in working relationships between individuals, and even entire functional groups, after they have participated together in training where they were required to work together. There is something about being on a four or five person team, preparing to make a presentation to a peer group of fifteen to twenty employees, that draws people together and eliminates the walls we normally find between areas of our organization.

Active class participation is vital in making the training effective. The lecture format is a definite 'no no'. Class participants should be just that – participating actively, becoming involved, learning by doing. Also this makes the learning fun and increases the likelihood of on-the-job application once employees have become comfortable in class with the various concepts and techniques.

Organizational problems identified by participants can many times be solved on the basis of these in-class discussions. For example, a nuclear aircraft carrier with a crew of over 5000 was trying to improve morale levels and focused on food service as a longstanding crew complaint. Imagine trying to feed and satisfy the tastes of over 5000 'employees' whose average age is 20! A crew menu committee had been formed but rarely was able to meet and address menu issues. When the problem was raised as part of a Quality training exercise, some rapid solutions resulted from lively class discussion and the 'brainstorming' that can occur in that environment.

QUALITY TRAINING LOGISTICS

Ideally, the class should be 15 to 20 in size. Obviously, a key variable is the availability of training rooms to accommodate these groups. One company had a series of smaller rooms that were used for training. This just required that they train additional instructors to accommodate the larger number of total training sessions. Another organization dedicated one training room five days a week, all day, for Quality training. Therefore, the size of the class is contingent upon the room size and the number of teams we want in each class.

Workshop teams should be limited in size to four to five people per team for maximum individual impact. If teams are larger, some individuals will 'hide' in the group and not participate fully. It is very hard to hide when you are with only three or four other team-mates. Moreover, there should probably not be more than three or four teams in a class. This will control the time spent on team presentations. These presentations are vital for effective training, but they can be time consuming and possibly unmanageable with more than four teams presenting.

The room itself should be set up in a 'U' shape. This allows easy and direct contact between class participants and does not allow for people to congregate in the last rows as invariably occurs with 'theater' style seating. We want everyone 'on the front line' and the 'U' shape also enables the instructor to move freely about the class and promote participation.

To maximize participation, a mix of audio-visual materials should be used. If the lecture format stifles participation, so does an over dependence on videos and the presentation of material via slides. Videos should be no longer than 15–20 minutes for maximum impact and information retention. Further, they should augment and complement the subject matter presented in other segments of the class. They should definitely not simply restate what has already been presented.

Transparencies – 'overheads' – are the most effective training tool for groups of this size where we want active participation. Transparencies enable us to present material clearly and visually in normal room lighting. They also allow us to easily re-present material when questions or clarification require it. On the other hand, slides require a darkened room and retracing our steps is an awkward and time-consuming affair.

It is also most impactful to move away from the overheads on occasion and utilize blackboards, dry-erase boards, and/or easel pads. This adds emphasis to points mentioned on the overheads and allows the instructor to 'customize' the training to the specific class. This 'customizing' is a vital component to effective training and maximizing participation. If the training is dealing with specific employee situations generated by the class, then attention and retention are maximized.

However, if the presentation is generic, bland, and seemingly programmed, than it will be received accordingly. All effective training must address itself to the key question in each participant's mind – 'What's in this for me?' We address this issue best by getting the class involved and working the training material into their environment, rather than vice versa.

The use of case studies dealing with some other organization's problems and experiences will have limited impact with most groups. Despite their intelligence and interest in the subject, most individuals are very focused on their own particular situation at the inception of Quality training. They want to see how Quality applies to them rather than how it applies to some other industry, no matter how closely related.

In time, participants will see that the problems experienced by most organizations are consistent from industry to industry. However, at the outset, focus your examples on their world. It is important to get the class participants to share their examples. The instructors should not feel they must have a repository of examples for every part of the organization.

If we address the specific issues of class participants, we will almost certainly guarantee their attention, participation, and thereby retention of the material presented.

IDENTIFY SPECIALIZED TRAINING NEEDS

While training an entire organization is no easy task, training special segments within the organization will pose particular difficulties. For example, how do we train a field sales force, our team of international auditors, or our engineers who are perpetually traveling? Clearly, every organization has within it groups that do not lend themselves to classic training schedules of one three hour class per week for four weeks, for example. Therefore, each organization will need to address their particular situations, but several guidelines can be considered.

First, some type of training is imperative for these 'special' people. They cannot be exempted or overlooked. In fact, many such groups

– particularly field sales people with their direct contact to our customers – play a critical role in our Quality Improvement efforts.

Secondly, they will probably require some condensed version of our standard training material. This could take the form of less breadth to the topics covered and more targeted presentations on topics particularly relevant to this group. Direct discussion with the management of this group will help establish the appropriate training needs.

Thirdly, they will probably have to be trained as a group, which is contrary to our objective of functionally mixed sessions, but possibly cannot be avoided.

Fourthly, they should be provided with 'pre-work' before the actual training to maximize the impact and retention of the material provided in the condensed training.

For example, one organization sent the actual training manuals to participants in its special training classes before the sessions and gave 'pre-reading' assignments. Other organizations developed a reading material packet with articles about Quality and Quality Improvement and asked that these be read prior to attending training.

A third organization assigned some 'pre-reading' and requested all participants be prepared to discuss a particular 'Quality' problem from their specific work process as part of the training session. This type of advance work maximizes the abbreviated sessions and moves the training from exposition to explanation and implementation rapidly.

A key part of any Quality training is the immediate application of what is learned in class to the actual workplace and an individual's job process. Therefore, in-class workshops and after class action assignments should deal with 'real-life' workplace problems and situations, rather than games or simulated case study scenarios.

Employee teams should select work processes to address and then apply their training to that actual process as the training progresses. Nothing reinforces the training more thoroughly than seeing the concepts successfully applied directly in front of you on a process you're familiar with. An effective way to reinforce the application of what is being learned is to have successful projects presented upon completion to the management board in a public forum where, at a minimum, organization managers are encouraged to attend and recognize the success of the presenters.

In one organization this approach not only produced excellent teamwork to address a nagging problem, but it also motivated previously reticent class participants to present their projects to their management board. In fact, one particular team spokesperson at a management board presentation was a female clerical employee who at the outset of training had requested that her class instructor never call upon her because of her fear of speaking to groups. Four weeks later, she was presenting to her grateful management board with a confidence and skill she had never before possessed or believed possible because of the team-building nature of the shared Quality training experience. If that was all she gained from her Quality training, then the training was a tremendous success, both from her vantage point and that of her management board.

TRAINING CONTENT – 'IF THEY LEARN ONLY ONE THING'

While every organization is different, and therefore should tailor its Quality training material to its own unique personality, certain issues have proven to be almost universally applicable. In this regard, we are often asked when reviewing the subject of Quality training, 'if our employees could learn only one thing in Quality training, what would it be?' In our experience the one subject that continually sparked the most interest and most enthusiastic application after the conclusion of training was a discussion of customer-focused process improvement. Here is what we tell them.

The first step in learning about customer needs and expectations is to understand that all work is a process – a series of actions that produce a customer desired output. Each department within an organization is involved in a series of processes. Examples of these processes could include new product development, teaching a class, inventory management, forecasting, launching an airplane from a carrier, accounts payable, admitting a patient to a hospital. These are large and extended processes that are difficult to understand and analyze until we start to understand their process flow.

Process flow is the graphic representation of a process from its inception to completion. Where does a particular process begin? Where does it end? It is very difficult to analyze a process in the hopes of improving it if we do not know what the total process looks like.

Think of an example in our personal life. We continually discover that we are 'bouncing' checks, yet we know that we have deposited sufficient funds in our bank account. What is the source of the problem? Lazy or stupid bank personnel who cannot credit our account properly? Before jumping to this type of conclusion, we need to examine the process flow involved in this process.

In this example, the process starts when we deposit a check into our checking account. We record that amount in our check book and even retain a copy of our deposit receipt. Then we write checks against this amount, yet they still bounce.

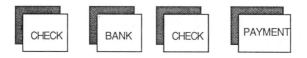

What we have failed to understand is that there is more to this process than we currently know. There is an important interim step in which our deposited check must 'clear' once it has been deposited. Also we need to understand that the bank will not pay against the check we draw on our account until the check clearing period is completed, so there is a time element involved.

Therefore, a picture of this process flow would include our depositing a check, the check clearing, and then our writing a check against our new, cleared balance. A picture of this process helps us to understand both the process flow and process management.

Process management helps us understand where 'things *can* go wrong' or 'where things *are* going wrong'. By diagramming an entire process we can start to analyze the problem areas and concentrate our efforts on those areas, rather than expending our efforts against a vast and undefined problem.

CHECKING

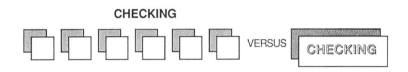

As we progress in the Quality Improvement process we will move from looking at the process areas that are *now* causing us problems to those which *might* prove problematic later. That is prevention – causing things not to happen, particularly bad things. With prevention as our strategy, we do not wait for problems to arise. We examine our processes, identify the areas where problems could arise, and then proactively address those areas to eliminate the potential problem sources.

Consider how we could apply process flow and process management to processes within our organization. Take new product development. Where does this process begin? What is the output of this process? What does the entire process look like, from start to finish?

Diagramming the new product development process may appear to be an enormous and time-consuming task, but we will gain an exceptional understanding of this process – and the opportunities for potential problems within this process – by conducting this exercise. Frankly, it is impossible to effectively and efficiently manage a process if we do not first understand its flow.

By understanding the process flow, we are also able to determine the cycle time for this process – how long does it take from start to finish? Understanding the cycle time for any process is critical if we are really serious about improving that process. Tom Peters and other business authors have continually emphasized that time – specifically cycle time – will represent an increasingly important strategic weapon.

87

If we can do something in one day that takes our competitor two days or one week, aren't we at a distinct competitive advantage? It may be apocryphal, but there is a well circulated Quality anecdote about cycle time and the renowned car maker, Volvo. The story goes that Volvo engineers were celebrating a significant engineering breakthrough by shortening the automobile model changeover time from six weeks to six days. (This is the amount of time necessary to retool and refit an automobile assembly line from one year's model to the new model.) This type of dramatic cycle time breakthrough would appear to have guaranteed Volvo a distinct competitive advantage for some time to come.

The enthusiasm of the Volvo engineers was brought to a screeching halt when it was determined that Toyota engineers had further shortened this cycle time from six days to six hours by providing workers conducting the assembly line changeover with uniforms that contained the actual tools they would need for their specific task in the changeover!

Whatever the organization or industry, we have an important piece of data when we know the cycle time of our key processes. If we know this information, we can measure it, track it, and seek to continuously improve it.

One way to directly address the improvement of our process cycle times is to determine through an examination of the process flow where in the process we are adding value and where we are only adding costs.

Studies across a number of industries and organizations have shown that the vast majority of activities regarding any process merely add cost. These are all the times where jobs or products are queued up waiting for the next part of the process, where they are being transported from one area to another, where they are waiting inspection or waiting transportation. The proportion of adding costs to adding value has been shown to be as high as 95% to 5%. Studies with Volvo demonstrate that their experience in auto assembly was very consistent with 95% of time being spent on cost adding activities and only 5% of the time on activities that add value.

While these relationships between adding value and adding cost are disturbing, it would be even more disturbing if we did not know what the relationship was in our organization! And the only way we will have this powerful information at our disposal is to conduct an analysis of our key processes starting with a very basic process flow or process mapping.

Numerous organizations have been able to make rapid improvements based upon this type of basic analysis because the results are so visible, and in many cases, so 'eye-opening'! One organization we studied added a 'geographic' element to their process flow analysis. They not only mapped out their key processes, but they also diagrammed how the products of these processes flowed across and through the organization.

It probably comes as no surprise – except to them – that they found products, reports, and planning documents were continually crisscrossing the organization's facilities, with vast amounts of time wasted in transit via interoffice mail. One simple decision to re-engineer their production floor to place consecutive operations contiguous to one another cut the cycle time for that one product by over 75%.

Hospitals are eagerly embracing the concept of cycle time reduction as they try to shorten patients' length of stay. They are discovering that this costly treatment cycle time can be significantly reduced through proper scheduling and effective communication between various departments within the hospital. How often have we been in the situation where we are waiting literally hours for procedures or consultations that are only minutes in length?

One hospital began to examine its various clinical procedures through a cycle time analysis and came to some startling awareness. They found that parts of the hospital ran according to their own rules and procedures, with little regard to the overall hospital objectives and no regard for the Patient-Customer. This hospital found that hip replacement operations conducted on Thursdays or later in the week entailed patients staying in the hospital at least until the following Tuesday, as the physical therapists who would work with the postoperative hip-replacement patients only worked on Tuesdays and Thursdays!

The short term solution to this problem was to reschedule hip-replacements for the first part of the week only. The longer term solution was to bring the physical therapists into the hospital community and convince them that their schedule should derive from the patients' needs, not vice versa. Again, this important and cost saving learning only occurred because an organization started with an examination of the process flow for one of its key processes!

With even the most basic mapping of a process, we can start to manage and analyze it so that we can actually determine what is taking place, what the cycle time of our process is, and where we are adding value or adding cost.

Let's apply these concepts of Process Flow and Process Management to another business example where problems have surfaced in numerous organizations – accounts payable.

A problem has arisen in the accounts payable group. They are spending an exceptional amount of time with incorrectly completed expense reports. We see the symptoms of this problem in several areas. The accounts payable group is incurring a great deal of overtime because of all the time spent checking, rechecking, returning, and reprocessing these expense reports.

Those submitting the expense reports are growing increasingly testy because they are not being reimbursed promptly and therefore are incurring penalty charges against their credit cards. The secretarial staff in both accounts payable and those departments submitting the expense reports are spending a great deal of time shuffling these same reports back and forth. Everyone is starting to blame the other and no one is talking directly to anyone.

Our first step in remedying this situation is to examine the process, not the people. Everyone is trying their best. Everyone is working hard. Unfortunately, all their hard work is not very productive and they are spending valuable time on rework. Our goal in this process is to have all expense reports produced and processed 'right the first time'.

What does the expense report process look like? Where does it start and where does it end? Let's diagram the process.

Once we have diagrammed the process flow, we can begin process management. Where are the problem areas within this process? These problem areas can potentially exist in each step of the process. Does the problem occur in our submitting the reports to our secretary for typing? In our review of the typed report? In our submission of this report to our supervisor?

Process management involves detective work in determining where problems are occurring. Let's say in this example that accounts payable is returning expense reports in most cases for lack of proper signatures. We are able to determine this through a simple ranking of reasons for returned reports. Therefore, we can concentrate our preliminary analysis on the process of submitting the expense report from our supervisor to accounts payable. That appears to be the problematic area, at least initially.

Now what?

Now we need to examine this specific, narrowly focused process of our supervisor submitting expense reports to accounts payable in greater detail. We do this by utilizing a powerful tool in Quality Improvement – the process model (Fig. 6.1).

The process model helps us examine processes in order to determine if the customer needs and expectations involved in the process are clear, understood, or if they even exist.

1. PROCESS SCOPE - Submit Expense Report to Accounts Payable Department.

2. OUTPUT - Completed Expense Report

3. CUSTOMER - Accounts Payable

Figure 6.1 The process model.

First, we need to determine the scope of the process we are examining. The key to effective use of the process model is to narrowly define the scope of the process under observation.

In our example, we are examining the process of our supervisor submitting an expense report to accounts payable. We can feel confident that we have effectively narrowed the scope of this process by the fact that the process has one output – an expense report. If we found that the process we were analyzing appeared to have more than one output, then we should go back and narrow the scope further.

With the scope of the process defined, and the output of the process established, we next need to determine the customer for this output. Who receives the output of our process? In our example, the customer is accounts payable.

Once we know the customer for our process' output, we can then establish the needs and expectations that the customer has for that output. Specifically, what does the customer want the output to look like? In this case, accounts payable has specific requirements for expense reports submitted for payment. These requirements represent their needs and expectations regarding the expense reports. One of these requirements is that expense reports be signed by the supervisor and the person initiating the report.

By using the process model we now have determined in a simple, step by step fashion following the numerical sequence outlined in Fig. 6.2, that while needs and expectations were established for this process, they were not clearly understood by all participants in the process. Therefore, there existed a gap that resulted in rework

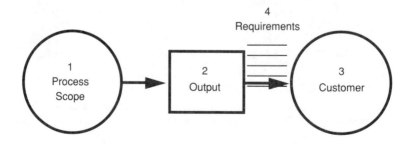

Figure 6.2 The step-by-step numerical sequence of the process model.

and some consternation to our employees. We can now move to address this gap through improved communication between accounts payable and those utilizing their services.

Accounts payable could also examine how long their current expense report process took and which steps in the process represented value added and which merely added cost. In fact, this examination determined that vast amounts of time in the process involved rewriting, re-routing, and reviewing expense reports with very little time in the process spent on value adding activities – like issuing our expense check!

This specific organization addressed this problem initially by putting the expense report system on an interoffice computer network which automatically checked the submissions for accuracy and electronically routed them to the appropriate management for approval. The expense checks were then processed and given to the employee. A future refinement under consideration will be the direct deposit of expense checks in employee bank accounts through electronic funds transfer, altogether eliminating the need for checks.

The process model is a tool in Quality Improvement and like all tools, it should be used in the correct situations for maximum effect. The process model is ideal when examining a problematic process, such as our accounts payable and expense report problem. Additionally, the process model can be used preventively when we are considering either new processes or changes to existing processes.

In each case, the process model can be used to examine the new process, or the process to be changed, and determine if we have considered the output of that process, the customer for that output, and what the customer wants from that output.

The time and effort spent proactively with an examination of process flow, process management, cycle time, value adding versus cost adding actions, and the process model will eliminate far greater amounts of time we currently spend reacting to problems after they occur. That is why customer-focused process improvement is the subject we stress with organizations if they are to learn 'only one thing' in Quality training.

Training is a major element in both the ISO 9000 standards and the Baldrige criteria, as might be expected. Both detail in some depth the importance of training for all levels of the organization. ISO 9000 places specific emphasis on various statistical techniques that are appropriate for certifying that our Quality effort is 'in control'. The Baldrige criteria emphasize the importance of training throughout the seven categories of this award. In fact, the Baldrige guidelines even require applicants to submit actual data referring to the type, level, and number of individuals trained, in both Quality and a variety of other related disciplines.

In conclusion, Quality training is probably the most intricate of all the Quality implementation actions. However, it is a process that will respond to effective planning, clear determination of the organization's needs, communication, and a prevention-oriented management style. It is an ideal opportunity to apply the techniques of Quality Improvement to its actual implementation.

IMPLEMENTATION ACTION 3: SUMMARY

Let's summarize the key actions in making Quality training happen.

1. Develop an overall plan for training the entire organization in Quality. This plan should include a timetable for the training, the locations for the training, the number of instructors required, and the actual training materials to be used.
2. Select a group of trainers from the organization. Look for individuals who excel in public presentations and are well-regarded by the organization. Who you pick as Quality training instructors will say a great deal about management's commitment and ownership of implementing Quality Improvement.
3. Determine the number of instructors required by considering the size of the organization, the number of training locations available, the length of the training course, and the amount of time in which you want the entire training completed.
4. Arrange the Quality training classes to be cross-functional, with as many levels represented in each class as the organization is comfortable with.

5. Set up training rooms in a 'U' format, with ideally not more than 20 per class.

6. Examine the organization for groups who will require special training, such as a field sales force, or those with special language requirements. Develop the appropriate training course for these individuals, so that they are a natural part of the process, not an exception.

7. Include in your Quality training materials key organizational elements that require clear communication. Such elements could include your organization's vision, mission, critical success factors, Quality implementation strategy, and recognition system.

8. Conduct pilot-test classes to determine if your initial approach to Quality training is achieving the desired results. This is prevention in action.

Implementation action 4 Management by fact: measurement and the cost of non-Quality

7

The modern organization is swamped with data. In fact, there is a data deluge where once there was a data dearth. Even the smallest organizations can have sophisticated information systems churning out reams of material thanks to the advent of the personal computer. Now the lap top version of this computer and the portable fax allow us to become mobile data centers – spewing ever more information across our organization.

But is all this data enhancing or encumbering our organization? Are we better informed or merely engulfed? Are we spending more time producing, printing, shipping and storing data than we spend analyzing it? Is the data we really need lost in a sea of useless or inactionable 'background noise'? Now that we have the capability to produce all this information, do we have the capacity to digest it, and more importantly, the courage to act upon it?

A case in point. Several major organizations receive monthly sales reviews the first Monday of each month. These printed tomes are three to four inches in depth and weigh several pounds. The companies' systems groups spend vast amounts of time at the end of each month to guarantee this material is loaded onto the computer and run over the weekend prior to the first Monday of each month. They have even made major capital appropriations for high-speed printers to accommodate these reports. Once printed these reports are then shrink-wrapped and delivered to offices before the start of business and sit waiting on desktops when managers arrive at their desks.

Invariably, everyone looks at this mountain of numbers, sighs, picks up the behemoth and unceremoniously deposits it in the nearest 'circular file'. Unopened, unread, unproductive. Yet, each month this scenario is repeated. Structural engineers have even expressed concern should all report recipients drop them into their waste baskets at the same time! Systems engineers wonder aloud why everyone needs 'hard copy' when every office has one, or more, personal computers.

So what does any of this have to do with Quality? Our goal in Quality Improvement is to efficiently and effectively build our business – to add value, not cost, to our processes. Clearly, unread, unused reports that consume valuable computer and printing time do not add value. Further, this is another example where we have not effectively determined the needs and expectations of an internal customer-supplier relationship. Who needs what and when? How do they want to see it? Rather, we have opted for the 'this is the monthly report, this is the way it's always been done' syndrome. It has become part of the woodwork of organizations – very expensive woodwork.

In fact, Quality Improvement is all about the *effective* use of data. It is impossible to 'improve' our Quality if we do not have effective and impactful data and measurement. However, the goal of our measurement efforts in Quality Improvement is to concentrate on the 'significant few' measures and disregard the 'trivial many'.

For example, if we are trying to lose weight, we need to measure our weight on a regular basis using consistent scales and measures. Our measure is pounds lost. However, we could judge our progress by how our clothes felt or the comments made by acquaintances. Or we could do a complete analysis of body dimension changes and trends. However, the simple scale and the process of a weekly weigh-in will meet our criteria of determining pounds lost. The other systems will merely confuse the process. When dealing with measurement and data it is best to remember the oft-forgotten adage: keep it simple.

So it is with our organization. Each functional area within the organization is responsible for a key process or processes.

98

This process, or processes, forms that function's reason for being. Clearly, any part of our organization which cannot identify its work process is an excellent candidate for a major cost saving effort!

Moreover, all processes are measurable in that they produce an output and receive inputs – all of which can be measured. It is the responsibility of each functional management to determine its key work process, the important criteria for each of these processes and then to measure performance versus these criteria. Management must then evaluate the effectiveness of these functional groups based upon their achievement of agreed upon targets or goals in these measurements.

Theoretically, that is what most organizations are doing today. We call it Management By Objectives (MBO). Yet, reality usually finds current measures or objectives to be vague, imprecise, non-quantifiable. Management confuses 'sloganeering' with strategy, so that corporate strategic statements tend towards the 'high-sounding', but are empty beneath the surface. How do you measure your results versus 'Quality is job one'? That makes evaluation equally vague and, at worst, subjective and qualitative. Additionally, these objectives can be counterproductive when one functional group's goals conflict with another's – lower inventory versus improved customer service, for example.

While each organization and the people within the organization should determine their key processes and what criteria to measure, management must orchestrate the entire effort, so conflicts are avoided. This orchestration should take the form of a clear delineation for the entire organization of the critical success factors we previously discussed.

Here are some examples of processes within a variety of functions that are being actively measured – and acted upon – by numerous organizations.

Marketing	performance, positive and negative, versus forecast; percent of sales volume sold at less than full revenue; new product launch cycle time.
Sales	orders returned; billing disputes; sales (units and monetary) per call.

Operations   manufacturing cycle time by product;
                 inventory levels;
                 order fill rate.

Finance   budget versus actual performance;
                 accounts receivable – days sales outstanding;
                 expedited freight and mail;
                 billing disputes.

Research   development cycle time;
                 regulatory questions, recalls, citations.

With this type of quantitative measure, we can also begin to clearly identify and prioritize our problems. No longer must our corrective efforts focus on the most immediate problem, or the person who screams the loudest. Now we can objectively evaluate our problem areas and quantify the problems.

We want our organization to be able to say, 'here is a problem, here is how often it occurs, and here is what it is costing our organization'. This type of basic skill will enable the organization to prioritize its activities and focus on the serious situations confronting the organization, rather than becoming swamped in a sea of non-quantified trivia.

THE COST OF NON-QUALITY

Our use of the cost of non-Quality will help in this process and enable us to not only quantify the occurrence of problems, but then to place a monetary value on them as well. This process should also be kept simple. It should *not* be our intent to capture every dollar, pound, and franc of non-Quality. Rather, we are looking for large numbers which help us place these various items in perspective. We should determine the monetary value of items being measured simply by calculating the time and material involved. Clearly, our time has a value and so does wasted material.

It is just that simple. We should also take into consideration what other impact to the organization certain problems cause and minimally capture them in our calculations. It is one thing to know that 30% of all expense reports have to be returned because they are improperly completed; it is quite another thing to then understand the actual cycle time of expense reports, the actual number of employees involved in processing the rework, and the time value of money lost through the delays. Suddenly a simple expense report problem is not so simple or unimportant any more!

Another classic problem which occurs monthly in organizations is the rush to ship products before month-end in order to credit these shipments to that month's sales figures. This practice is particularly intense at the end of each quarter and becomes a monumental headache at the end of a fiscal year when the organization is struggling to make its sales forecast. Invariably, the entire organization – and particularly the warehouse and finance operations – are put through the wringer to expedite these shipments. Extra shifts, round the clock schedules, and shortcuts abound!

Management knows that this is taking place and may even be the source of the problem, but when all they hear is moaning about this problem, then they are unlikely to see it as a problem. If we are now able to quantifiably show them the extent and cost of this process, then we have an excellent opportunity to correct the situation and get to the root cause of a problem versus just addressing its symptoms.

Thus we can replace the old debate of whose problem is the more serious with an objective, quantitative ranking – 'here are our problems, here is how often they occur, here is what they are costing us'. That is information we can act upon and allocate resources based upon.

The ability to act upon these problems cannot be underestimated. When management realizes what its problems are actually costing and when it sees the frequency with which they are occurring, the organization is quite likely to receive the suppport for the necessary corrective action.

For example, several companies determined through measurement that their marketing personnel were spending over 30% of their time on budget and forecast revisions. They also determined that the level of accounts receivable was steadily rising and that inventory levels were also on the increase, despite official pronouncement about the need to reduce both.

Clearly, measurement is not going to solve these problems, but effective and targeted measurement will highlight the areas requiring immediate attention and then let us know about the relative success of our corrective efforts.

Measurement is critical to all types of organizations. There is an ongoing debate about the cost of public education in the US as communities find themselves faced with growing tax bills to pay for this service, yet the educational community is unable or unwilling to provide any clear measures as to what they are providing. Several school boards are now developing quantifiable measures of the performance of their school systems so that they can determine if progress is really occurring and if the local taxpayers are really receiving any type of return for their investment.

Or take the case of a senior marketing executive at a major US company who doubted the need for measurement in Quality Improvement, 'we're in Marketing, we're measuring things all the time, and nothing is improving, so what's the big deal about measurement?' Translate this to our personal life, weight loss example: 'hey, I'm weighing myself everyday and I haven't lost a pound yet. Measurement doesn't work!' And it won't work unless the scale you are using is ten flights of stairs up and there's no elevator! Measurement is the thermometer – it tells us we have a fever. It is then up to us to take the appropriate and needed action.

THE ROLE OF CHARTING IN MEASUREMENT

A key component to measurement is charting. Many times the two terms are used interchangeably and they really should not be. We can measure data via columns of numbers. However, charting adds a visual impact to the data that illuminates where raw data can often hide trends. Charting can visually emphasize trends, relationships, and data patterns. Additionally, charts can tell a story with little additional need for accompanying text.

For example, take our earlier discussion of Balance of Trade trends and the relative strength or weakness of the US dollar. One chart showing both items debunks the belief that a weak dollar will bring an improved Balance of Trade.

Or consider the example of a major manufacturer with significantly premium priced products compared to their closest competitor.

Everyone knew and accepted the premium price level internally until the trend of this price premium (increasing) was charted over time and compared with market share (decreasing sharply) during the same period. The company management radically revised its pricing strategy based upon the results portrayed in this charting exercise. Mere numbers alone did not have the dramatic impact of a well presented chart. Management had seen both sets of numbers before, but never graphically presented together. Once the graphs were presented, little discussion was necessary and real action occurred as prices were immediately frozen and a price rollback planned.

Charting also has other benefits. Organizationally, it demonstrates commitment to Quality Improvement and fosters a team spirit. Employees can walk around the organization and see functional areas and work groups pulling together to address the key business processes they have selected to measure and improve. Additionally, the charting effort feeds upon successes. It communicates by its mere presence that, yes problems exist, but that they are being addressed. That is really all an organization needs to see. What they fear most is that all the problems they see on a daily basis are going unnoticed and unaddressed by management.

Finally, public charting tells visitors – including our suppliers – that we are serious about Quality and expect them to adopt the same attitude.

A QUALITY CHART EXAMPLE

The actual charts used for our measurement effort should be simple and straighforward. It is strongly advised to have one format for the entire organization. This provides a uniform look to the chart itself, although the information charted will vary by process.

This format is simple, yet flexible and is in use by numerous organizations. Here are some important points on its effective use.

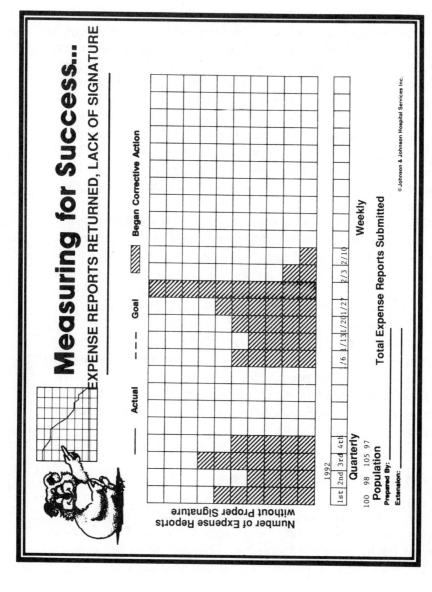

Figure 7.1 An example of a Quality chart – expense reports returned without a proper signature.

1. Once we have determined what item we are going to measure, we need to determine the mechanics of developing our measurement chart.

2. Start with the title. Keep it *simple*. If we are measuring expense reports submitted without proper signature because we have determined that this is the leading problem in our finance department, then our chart title would be: 'Expense reports returned for lack of signature'. Anyone reading that chart title would know exactly what we were measuring.

3. Determine our item measured and fill this in on the vertical line next to the left side graph. In our example, we would fill in: 'Number of expense reports without proper signature'. This provides a description of the numbers we will be reporting. Therefore, we will know if we are looking at 'eachs', percentages, etc.

4. Choose the time frame for our measurement. Possibly, we will use the smaller graph for a consolidation of data – monthly, quarterly, etc. Then we would use the right side graph for reporting the data more frequently – daily, weekly, etc. We would then consolidate this data into the left side chart at the appropriate time.

   Another use of the two charts is pre and post measurement. For example, we could use the left graph for historical (pre) data and the right graph for current (post) data.

   In our example, the left graph could be used to reflect the number of expense reports returned for lack of signature *before* we took corrective action. The right graph could then be used to report the results after (post) our corrective action. This type of measurement would enable us to learn if our corrective action were successful, or if we need to implement additional corrective action.

5. Next, choose the levels which will be marked along the vertical axis. Remember these will vary according to our time frame. For example, in our weekly graph, the ascending lines may be by '2s' – 2, 4, 6, 8, etc. expense reports returned for lack of signature. However, in the quarterly consolidation, the ascending lines may be by '10s' – 10, 20, 30, 40, etc.

6. Our next step is to fill in the date line. Again, this is a function of our selected time frame. Our consolidated quarterly report would have the appropriate quarters reported on this line, while our

weekly report would have the calender weeks – 2/14, 2/21, etc; – reported in the correct space. We put these time frames into words in the time period line.

7. The population line details the total sample from which your non-conforming items were selected. For example, if we process a total of 25 expense reports each week and from this total some number are returned for lack of signature, then our population would be 25 on our weekly chart. The quarterly consolidation population would be the sum of the weekly populations for the appropriate quarters.

8. The population measured line is merely the verbalization of the numbers reported on the population line. Remember the importance of communication in Quality Improvement. By writing out our time periods, item measured, and population measured, anyone could look at our measurement chart and understand what was happening.

BENCHMARKING AND MEASUREMENT

Measurement and the price of non-Quality can now provide our organization with a quantitative analysis of where we have been and where we are now. With this information in hand, we can begin to plan on where we should be going after today. This is the real basis of management by fact – our actions are being guided by objective measures rather than by subjective whims.

But how do we get from where we are today on any given measure to where we want to be tomorrow? And how do we determine what our continuous improvement goals should be; isn't steady progress against these goals enough?

It is at this juncture – once an organization has developed its critical success factors and begun measuring their progress toward achieving these factors – that benchmarking should be introduced to the organization, if it is not already an accepted organizational practice.

The preeminent practitioner of benchmarking in the world today is the Xerox Corporation and this organization defines benchmarking as 'the continuous process of measuring our product, services, and practices against our toughest competitors or those companies renowned as the leaders.'[1] A detailed discussion of benchmarking is available from a variety of excellent sources, notably Xerox's *Leadership Through Quality* series and Robert C. Camp's book, *Benchmarking – The Search for Industry Best Practices That Lead to Superior Performance*. These two works cover the subject of benchmarking in detail. However, it is appropriate here to highlight some of the important benchmarking lessons learned by organizations that have already had extensive experience with this important business practice.

FOCUS BENCHMARKING EFFORTS

It is critically important to focus our organization's benchmarking efforts. We have already developed our Critical Success Factors and our measures of the key processes related to these factors. Our benchmarking must focus on a prioritized few of these processes, not all of them. Benchmarking can be exceptionally worthwhile for an organization, but trying to benchmark too many processes at too macro a level at one time will represent a serious resource drain to our organization.

For example, a major hospital determined that its customer focused Critical Success Factors directly related to four items:

1. patient admissions process;
2. food service;
3. cancer care and treatment;
4. emergency room.

The hospital's management determined that all four should be benchmarked to determine the 'best in class' practices in each area, in order to provide targets for their continuous improvement efforts. A very noble objective, but highly impractical because each of these four areas represents an enormous structure of individual processes, each of which could represent an individual benchmarking project.

Specifically, food service is far too general an area to benchmark. Rather, the individual processes that make up food service first need to be prioritized by customer perceived importance. These processes could include: meal preparation; meal delivery; menu selection; ingredient ordering; patient satisfaction with the food service, etc.

UNDERSTAND OUR PROCESS FIRST

Once a specific process has been identified for benchmarking, it is critical to completely understand the functioning of our organization's own process before we examine and benchmark another organization's efforts. Only by thoroughly understanding our efforts can we truly know what to look for and ask about when we conduct a formal benchmarking project. This thorough understanding should include a complete comprehension of our process from start to finish. (A specific approach to this process examination is detailed in Chapter 6.) At minimum, we must have completely determined the process flow, cycle time, value and cost adding process steps, process personnel requirements, process outputs, and process customer(s). Armed with this knowledge at a minimum, we can intelligently benchmark our process versus that of another organization.

BENCHMARK PROCESSES, NOT RESULTS

It is very important that we understand that our benchmarking focuses on a process. We are not benchmarking results. Many organizations make the classic benchmarking error of 'benchmarking' results – comparing numbers from our organization to numbers from another organization or from a composite of several supposedly similar organizations. Tragically, numerous large and ostensibly reputable consulting firms aid and abet this error by providing – for a substantial fee – these benchmark numbers.

The fallacy in results benchmarking is that this comparison is worthless unless we thoroughly understand the process that generated those results. How can we compare the cost of our field sales force, for example, to another organization's unless we understand the duties performed by each? The benchmarking of results is based on the severely flawed logic that processes are comparable – if not

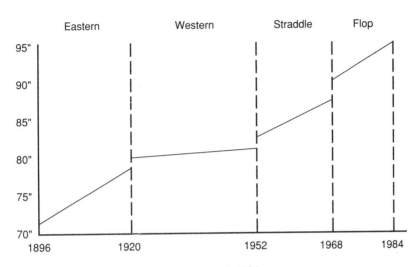

Figure 7.2 Olympic high jump records, 1896–1984.

identical – from one organization to another, if not from industry to industry. Of course, this is just not true.

Moreover, merely examining results will not provide the key end product of benchmarking – the knowledge of what process and specific activities relating to that process – result in 'best-in-class' performance. It is very probable that we will not be able to achieve 'best-in-class' results with our current process. Therefore, we will never learn that unless we understand the process that generated those best-in-class results.

The mistake of merely benchmarking results can be seen if we examine the historical world records achieved in the track and field event of high jumping (see Fig. 7.2). In fact, this event is a classic example of the implementation of basic Quality Improvement concepts to a non-business practice. Process management, measurement, continuous improvement, and benchmarking are all integral to this event.

Clearly, the high jumping techniques of 1990 are not the same techniques of 1900. In fact, you cannot physically achieve the current World Record heights of the 1990s with the 1900s 'scissor kick' technique. Process management and process improvement –

109

technique changes – have led to the dramatic improvement in World and Olympic records. Measurement has been used to record these results and demonstrate the benefits of the various process improvements. The high jump process has been continuously dissected by coaches and jumpers and its various process elements examined, challenged, compared, improved, or discarded in an effort for continuous improvement.

Moreover, coaches and jumpers continuously benchmarked the techniques of the best-in-class jumpers and adapted or modified these techniques – processes – to their advantage. Thus, when Dick Fosbury showcased the radically different and revolutionary 'Fosbury Flop' technique at the 1968 Oympics, coaches and jumpers around the globe benchmarked this technique against their own and moved almost entirely away from the western roll and straddle techniques that preceded the Fosbury Flop. If they had merely benchmarked results, they would never have achieved these new heights!

BENCHMARK THE 'BEST-IN-CLASS'

Many organizations are satisfied to limit benchmark efforts to their industry. Often this is not a conscious decision. Rather, we believe our industry is unique, with situations entirely its own, and that no other industry has any knowledge to offer us. This attitude is a guarantee for limited short-term success and inevitable long-term failure. Rather, we must look beyond our industry to other industries with related, though not necessarily identical, processes. What can we learn from their expertise that we can apply to our industry? Those who will win the Quality revolution will be open and receptive to these cross-industry comparisons.

Take as an example a hospital that identified patient admission as one of its critical success factors. After fully documenting and understanding their own admissions process, a decision was made not to benchmark other hospital admissions practices. This exercise could have provided the false sense of security derived from knowing no one in our industry is better at any specific process than we are. That is when we invariably 'rest on our laurels' and lay the groundwork for eventual marketplace disaster.

However, this hospital realized from customer feedback and research that all hospitals did a relatively poor job in the patient admissions process. Therefore, if we limited ourselves to this industry, our standards could be artificially low. Rather, this hospital sought out the industry that admitted customers (patients) better than anyone else. They determined that luxury hotels did this best and that specific hotels had achieved 'best-in-class' practices. Certainly, hospitals and luxury hotels are significantly different in many ways. But the real business building learning in benchmarking comes from seeing where the similarities exist and then garnering the process knowledge from these 'best-in-class' practices.

Therefore, this hospital benchmarked its admissions process against the check-in process of various luxury hotels and made dramatic improvement in a process that customers had identified as one of the most critical to their satisfaction with hospitals. By making this cross-industry benchmarking effort, the hospital achieved a substantial advantage versus its competitors and this advantage translated directly to the hospital's business results and overall success.

BENCHMARKING AND THE INNOVATION TRAP

The great benefit of benchmarking is being able to learn the best-in-class practices from their practitioners and adapt them to our organization. This is both a benefit and a potential trap. Continuing our track and field analogy, we can learn the Fosbury Flop and improve our high jump results with some dedicated practice. And when the next technique improvement comes along, we can adapt that as well. But we can see the trap in this line of reasoning – we are always going to be the second into the market, at best! Who remembers the second person to fly alone across the Atlantic after Lindbergh or the second to climb Mount Everest?

Therefore, what we really need to benchmark and adapt for our organization is the environment that fostered these innovations. What prompted, stimulated, encouraged, and challenged Dick Fosbury to dramatically alter the accepted high jump techniques? Whatever that muse was, we need to bottle it and infuse our organization with it,

111

because our real goal is to become the benchmark – the best-in-class practitioner – that other organizations benchmark, rather than continually benchmarking others.

Measurement is an integral topic in both the ISO 9000 standards and in the Baldrige National Quality Award criteria. Probably no single topic receives more attention in either of these Quality guidelines than does measurement for the simple reason that it is impossible to judge our progress towards Quality unless we measure that progress.

It is impossible to even attempt ISO 9000 certification without extensive measurements of other key processes within our organization. Moreover, the Baldrige criteria place a special emphasis throughout on the need to benchmark our measures, so that we not only determine our level of results, but can then compare that level to others within our industry and to the best-in-class. The cost of non-Quality is not a major element in either standard, but it is tremendously important internally to demonstrate our return on investment and to prioritize our resources.

In closing, it is important to continually remind ourselves that measurement will not solve our problems and developing a cost of non-Quality for these problems does not mean we are necessarily going to drop all that money to our bottom line. However, our measurement and cost of non-Quality efforts tell us – and our entire organization – how frequently our problems occur and what they are costing us. In turn this demonstrates what an opportunity we have for saving – or avoiding – these costs if we take effective corrective action.

IMPLEMENTATION ACTION 4: SUMMARY

Let's summarize the key actions in our fourth implementation action, measurement and the cost of non-Quality.

1. Assign implementation of this action to a member of the management board. Many times the chief financial officer assumes responsibility for measurement and the cost of non-Quality.

2. Have each functional group determine their key work processes. These will be, or certainly should be, the processes management holds them accountable for in the organization's annual plan. These are the processes that each group should measure and benchmark once they are fully documented and understood.

3. Develop an organization-wide measurement chart format. Make supplies of these charts available to the management of each area. Develop both a large format for posting on the wall and a smaller, desk size version.

4. Determine that our Quality training program includes a discussion of measurement and the cost of non-Quality. Make certain that this discussion demonstrates our measurement charts and how to use them.

5. Monitor the use of public measurement charts by the organization and recognize those groups that are actively participating in measurement. Additionally, recognize those who are making real progress at lowering their cost of non-Quality, particularly on items impacting external customers.

6. Remember that measurement and the cost of non-Quality are tools and represent a means to an end. They are not the 'end'. Do not institute a 'measurement police' that checks to see who is measuring and who is not. The organization will determine the key elements to measure. The measurement committee, directed by the management board member responsible for this action, can serve as consultants should any group within the organization have difficulty determining what to measure.

REFERENCE

[1] Xerox Corporation (1987) *Leadership Through Quality*, Xerox Corporation, Stamford, Connecticut, p. 11.

Implementation action 5
Corrective action

8

Effective, institutionalized corrective action is a vital component to Quality Improvement. Corrective action must become an integral part of our organization's culture. We can no longer see problem areas or processes as an acceptable or normal part of business. Business can no longer be seen as a random series of problems which arise and to which we must react, 'hopping from fire to fire, from crisis to crisis'.

Rather, our organization – starting at the top – must adopt the attitude that all problems can be prevented and that the problems that occur must be attacked, solved, and their causes eliminated forever. Additionally, the organization must determine that this corrective action effort will be accomplished through teamwork, for the common good of the entire organization, not the greater glory of one functional group, or one individual, at the expense of others.

It is of paramount importance to understand that Quality Improvement is not problem solving. Many managers confuse Quality Improvement with a tool kit of problem-solving techniques – the more complicated, the better. Rather, Quality Improvement is about communication and prevention. Our goal is to prevent problems, not just solve them. We prevent them by anticipating, understanding, and managing our processes and continually communicating with our customers and suppliers to establish and conform to clear expectations.

But what do we do about all the problems that currently confront us? How is Quality Improvement going to help to eliminate those existing hassles?

Importantly, Quality Improvement is not going to do anything about eliminating our current problems. Rather, *we* are going to eliminate these problems forever by putting into practice the basic concepts of Quality Improvement. We are going to eliminate these problems forever by addressing them in a systematic method and pursuing them with our attitude of continuous improvement.

An important tool in the Quality Improvement process is the five part problem elimination model. This model pursues problem elimination in a systematic process. The model is outlined in Fig. 8.1.

This model is a straightforward, common sense approach to eliminating problems. It was developed by a consumer products company outside London, but it is applicable to any industry in any location. The model is not magic and the success we achieve with it is entirely dependent upon our efforts in accurately and completely addressing each step in the process. Importantly, it is *not* the model that is important, but rather the mental process that accompanies each of the five steps in the model.

Let's examine each step individually.

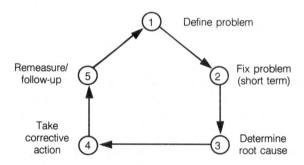

Figure 8.1 The problem elimination model.

DEFINE THE PROBLEM

Defining the problem may seem the easiest part of this process. It can be, if we focus on *defining* the problem. However, in developing our problem definitions we often include symptoms, use subjective evaluations, and/or bring personalities into the equation.

116

Our goal in defining the problem is to develop a definition which cannot be misunderstood or misinterpreted, and accurately presents the problem. We already have two important tools at our disposal that can assist us in clearly and accurately defining the problem – measurement and the cost of non-Quality. We can measure how often the problem occurs and we can report what this problem is costing our organization. In doing so, we have a clear picture that is non-controversial and separates people from the process.

Let's examine a real world example. Our finance department is having ongoing problems in accounts payable concerning employee's expense reports. Expense reports are being returned to employees for rework because the expense reports are not properly completed. Measurement helped us prioritize this problem and we even developed a measurement chart for it in Chapter 7.

We could also have used a pareto analysis, or stacking, of accounts payable department problems (Fig. 8.2). Not only did this pareto analysis help us determine expense reports as a problem, it pointed out the specific problem areas when we pursued the analysis further. Again, some detective work is often necessary to solve the mysteries confronting us at work.

Through this pareto analysis we have narrowed the focus of our problem. It is no longer an expense report problem. It is a clearly delineated problem we can intelligently attack and measurement was key to unravelling the problem. Now we can take some corrective action on the problematic areas within our expense reports process and then continue measurement to determine the success of our corrective action.

In our expense report problem with accounts payable, our measurement of this problem clearly details that 100 expense reports had to be reworked out of the 200 processed in January. We could further detail this definition by attributing a total cost to this rework. We can calculate this based upon the average time involved in the rework multiplied by the hourly wage rate of the personnel involved in the process.

117

Accounts payable problem areas
(incidents reported per month)

1. Expense reports returned   100
2. Supplier invoices returned   40
3. Credit notes sent   30

Reasons for expense report rework
(per 100 reworked reports)

1. No signature   70
2. Does not add   30
3. No/improper receipts   10
4. Miscellaneous   5

Nonsignature sources
(per 70 returned reports)

1. Supervisor   50
2. Employee   20
3. Both   10

Department source of nonsignature
(per 50 supervisor reports)

1. Marketing   30
2. Sales   15
3. Research   5

Figure 8.2 A pareto analysis of the accounts payable department problems.

Our next element in clearly defining the problem is to determine who needs to be involved in eliminating it. Specifically, what departments and/or individuals are involved in or are affected by this process? Clearly, these individuals will need to play some role in eliminating this problem forever, if only to be informed concerning how we may have modified the process. An aid in determining who is involved in the process is our analysis of process flow. This will point out where the process begins, where it ends, and who is impacted by it.

A process flow analysis can be accomplished through a very basic mapping of a process – what steps occur in what sequence? This need not be a complicated engineering exercise. Remember, keep it simple for the best and quickest results!

118

Once we have determined who needs to be involved in eliminating the problem, we need to ask ourselves two basic questions concerning the problem itself.

First, when will we feel confident that the problem has really been eliminated? Specifically, what is our measure of success? Secondly, when do we want to have a clearer picture concerning the real definition of this problem? We call this the definition date – the date by which we have clearly defined the problem and developed a plan of action to address it. The definition date is not when the problem has been eliminated, but rather the date when we have clearly defined it and have a plan developed to eliminate it.

Returning again to our accounts payable problem, their measure of success could be two consecutive months with no expense reports returned for reprocessing due to lack of signature. We would feel confident at that time that whatever corrective action we had taken had addressed the problem and eliminated it.

Additionally, accounts payable may determine that their definition date for this specific item is two weeks. We want to have a plan developed within two weeks in which the problem is clearly defined and a method for attacking it delineated. At the end of this two week period we may determine that additional time is required. However, we are serious about resolving this situation and therefore are unwilling to allow our definition date to continually slip.

FIX THE PROBLEM

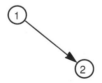

Fixing a problem involves the short-term actions we take to keep our process working and our operation in business. Unfortunately, we many times find ourselves caught in a 'define and fix' trap. This leads to fire-fighting, where we continually jump from one problem to the next without ever adequately resolving each one. Our excuse is that we never have enough time, but we will always have enough time to fight that fire when it erupts again.

However, fixing is a legitimate part of our problem elimination model. In fixing we need to determine how we are going to deal in the short term with the problem. Are we going to rework it, scrap it, or deviate it? None of these are options that we should be willing to accept for any length of time. Our attitude of continuous improvement would prevent us from doing so.

In accounts payable, we have been reprocessing the problematic expense reports. In other parts of our organization we have a deviation process where the problematic products or services are deviated on a temporary basis. In other instances, we may have to scrap the problematic items.

ROOT CAUSE IDENTIFICATION

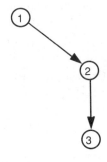

The root cause of a problem is that element which, when removed, will eliminate the problem entirely. Let's examine a real business example.

Several organizations we studied have experienced mold problems with some of their products. These organizations were able to define the problem by determining the amount and value of the product affected and deciding which parts of the organization needed to be involved. They also determined a measure of success and picked a definition date. They were then faced with the detective work of identifying the root cause of the mold. There are a variety of tools which can be brought to bear in this detective work.

The first is basic detective work – a question and answer process. This is a comparison of conforming and nonconforming outputs. You can use the various questions a detective might ask to assist with this analysis. Specifically, *where* were the two outputs produced, with *what equipment*, during *what time period* (shift), by *what work group*, with *what level of training*, following *what procedures*, and utilizing *what inputs*? These are just a sample of the questions that can be asked. It is very possible that this question and answer process will isolate the root cause.

In the mold example, several of the instances had inconsistent procedures as the root cause. Specifically, certain suppliers were following procedures while others were shortcutting the procedures for the sake of schedule. The products affected by the mold were all found to come from the suppliers not following the stated procedures.

Another tool for root cause identification is reviewing agreed upon expectations. Here we can review the customer's expectations to determine if all the expectations are established, agreed upon, clearly communicated, and met, or exceeded. We may find that this is not the case and therefore the source of the problem may be identified.

Charting is another possible tool for identifying the root cause. Is the problem occurring in a consistent pattern, in a repeating cycle, at specific intervals? These may all be determined from an analysis of measurement charts relating to the problem.

It is important to remember that the charts themselves will not solve our problems. We must be charting the correct items, in the proper format, to correctly identify our problem's root cause.

For example, the training section of an organization's human resources department was charting absences from training classes. Charting the total absences on a weekly basis showed a consistent pattern of missed classes but give no indication concerning the root cause. However, when the problem was measured on a daily basis, it became clear that the weekly totals were being driven by absences from classes conducted on Monday mornings and Friday afternoons. Once these classes were rescheduled to more user-friendly time periods, there were no subsequent absence problems.

The key lesson learned in this case was that the initial measurement – total absences per week – did not provide any more than surface information. It required a more in-depth study of the data – absences by day of the week – to uncover the real root cause of the problem. The people involved with the process – in this case those actually conducting the training classes – are an ideal source for determining what measure should be charted.

Brainstorming is another important tool for use in determining potential root causes. Those involved in the process should consider what could cause the problem, just as they can assist in determining the proper items to measure and chart. It is always important to include in these discussions those directly involved with the process. We call this 'ask the experts'. An understanding of the process flow is also vital for brainstorming to be an effective tool so that participants are dealing with a common view of the process. Experiments and tests can be used to prove or disprove the possibilities raised.

The key is to generate alternatives that one person or small group alone might not have considered. It is critical in brainstorming to allow for a free flow of ideas. There are no wrong answers or bad ideas in these sessions. What may seem a crazy idea when first introduced may in fact prompt a corollary idea from another participant that identifies the actual root cause of our problem. A good facilitator is vital to the successful use of brainstorming.

One final source for information on the root cause is statistical process control. This type of analysis will enable those involved in the process to determine two key points. First, is the process capable – can it produce the desired product or service? Secondly, is it is controllable – can we 'fine tune' the process – and what learning can be obtained from the problematic outputs of the process. It is important to remember that, in many instances, statistical process control does not require substantial quantitative skills. Many statistical process control tools are part of our everyday arsenal. Others are more specialized and can be very useful when applied in the proper situation.

TAKE CORRECTIVE ACTION

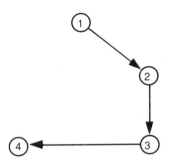

The corrective action taken should have as its objective the permanent elimination of the identified root cause. To be successful, the corrective action must be implementable, efficient (investment versus return should be considered), formally established, and clearly communicated to all involved in the process. Additionally, it is important to determine that the corrective action is not causing an entirely new problem. We are not being very efficient or effective if we merely trade one problem for another.

Therefore, it is appropriate to test our corrective action. This is consistent with our prevention orientation.

Once we have proven the effectiveness and efficiency of the corrective action, we need to make certain that it is thoroughly integrated into our process. This may involve changes to procedures, written communications, retraining of personnel, and generally a re-examination of our process. We call this closed loop corrective action. Everyone involved with the process is informed. We need to answer all the who, what, why, when, and how questions regarding a process change or modification.

REMEASURE AND FOLLOW-UP

How do we know that our corrective action has eliminated our defined problem? In the definition step we used measurement as one way to define the problem. We also determined a measure of success. In

123

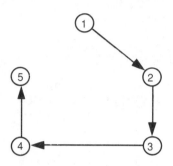

the remeasure step we bring both of these elements into play once more. First, we continue to measure our process. Is the problem still present? Have we achieved our measure of success? Quite simply, we used measurement to help us define the problem, we will now use measurement to determine its continued existence.

Follow-up involves a change to our process that guarantees that the corrective action taken to eliminate the problem remains in place. This follow-up can take two general forms – mistake proofing and process auditing.

Mistake proofing involves developing processes or systems which guarantee that a problem will not occur. We can think of many instances in our personal lives – all of which were probably put into place because of the existence of previous problems. For example, at the gas station we cannot put regular gas into our unleaded gas car because the pump nozzle and gas tank opening have been designed to be incompatible. This is an example of mistake proofing by *contact*.

Another example of mistake proofing is fill weight indicators. These indicators will not let a product pass until it meets the required fill weight. This is an example of mistake proofing by *automation*.

Many cars cannot be started unless the transmission is in park. Some standard transmission cars require that the transmission be in neutral and the clutch depressed before the car can be started. These are examples of mistake proofing by *action sequence*. Specifically, a particular sequence of actions must take place before a process can be initiated. Logging onto a computer is another example of action sequence mistake proofing.

124

A final example of mistake proofing is artificial intelligence. The 'Spell-Check' function in our computer software is an example of artificial intelligence. However, brainstorming with a secretarial group identified for us that it is possible for a word to be spelled correctly but still improperly used, so we must not rely entirely on artificial intelligence (we cannot be *two* careful!)

When we think of auditing, we invariably picture green eye-shades and people pouring over columns of numbers. This is results auditing. In this instance inspectors are auditing the finished product – our financial results. This type of results auditing is the same as inspection – the traditional Quality assurance or Quality control paradigm. Inspectors are merely sorting the good from the bad, and the cost of the bad products will have to be absorbed by the good ones.

Auditing in Quality Improvement involves auditing the process. Is the process capable – can it produce the expected output? Is it controllable – is it producing the expected output consistently or are these 'conforming' outputs occurring purely at random? Statistical process control is an excellent process auditing tool in that it identifies whether a process is in control or behaving completely at random.

Our goal in Quality Improvement is to prevent problems before they occur. Quality Improvement is not a problem-solving process. However, as we move to prevention, we need to eliminate the problems that exist in our processes today. The problem elimination model provides a structured manner for addressing these problems. Using the problem elimination model in addition to, or in conjunction with, other problem solving techniques will guarantee that we can eliminate our problems forever, thereby providing continually better products and services to our customers.

The problem elimination model provides a *process* for corrective action. Actually using this tool and the concomitant thought process is the responsibility of managers in all functions. Corrective action must start with teams of employees addressing a shared problem. Management can support them, provide the proper environment, and even the necessary resources. Most importantly, they can encourage employees to take corrective action and they can pitch-in, roll up their sleeves and get involved where appropriate.

When approaching the development of a corrective action system, many organizations reflect their basic tendency toward adding bureaucracy and adding cost, rather than adding value. Many organizations have developed formal corrective action systems that are *form driven*. This type of system has employees fill out forms delineating the problem, identifying responsible parties (or those believed responsible by the individual filling out the form), suggesting possible solutions to the identified problem, and several other factors.

The employees then route this form through some type of processing system. Copies of the original form are kept along the way for reference, logged into computer reporting systems, and printed out on a monthly status report. If corrective action ever takes place, it might be handled by some group not directly involved with the individual or group that originally reported the problem.

This form driven process of corrective action misses out on efficiency and effectiveness because it focuses on a *reporting* process, not on *resolving* a specific problem. It should not be our goal to develop an intricate reporting system for corrective action projects. Rather, it should be our goal to eliminate problems forever and start preventing their reoccurrence. Therefore, avoid a form *driven* corrective action process.

Several organizations have developed an effective and useful form which is used as an information vehicle in corrective action, rather than as a tracking-reporting vehicle. This form follows the five step problem elimination model and helps guide the corrective action process. Further, it serves as a repository of information which can be shared with those involved in the corrective action effort. The key point with this form is that it is a means to an end, whereas form driven processes make the form an end in the process.

Additionally, this recommended form can be circulated to our organization's management for possible recognition or sent to our awareness group for publication to the entire organization when completed at the conclusion of the corrective action project.

Some organizations we studied recognized the shortcomings of a form driven corrective action process and sought a better solution. They found that a great many corrective action projects were spawned as part of their Quality training. Teams would form in class to address specific company problems and these teams would

126

attack the problems with the tools they learned during each successive week of Quality training. However, it was feared that graduation from Quality training would eliminate the focus on the problem areas, as people slipped back into their day-to-day habits.

Therefore, the concept of a corrective action facilitator was developed. This individual would replace the in-class Quality training instructor who focused the classes on addressing workplace problems as part of Quality training. It would be the role of the corrective action facilitator to maintain this focus on significant organizational corrective action projects once the formal training phase is completed.

Corrective action facilitators would be volunteers from throughout our organization. Corrective action teams that had been formed to address a significant problem could request a facilitator through the corrective action committee. Facilitators should be limited to participation on two projects at any one time, so as not to overburden these employees who also had their own jobs to pursue.

The following is a description of the Corrective Action Facilitator as developed by one of the organizations successfully utilizing this corrective action technique.

The job of the corrective action facilitator is to assist teams, task forces, and/or sub-committees developed to undertake corrective action on a specific problem area or process. The facilitator would provide assistance concerning areas of team mechanics, meeting effectiveness, and Quality Improvement.

Team mechanics
The facilitator assists by ensuring that the team has a chairperson and that the process under review has a clear and defined 'owner'. The 'owner' of the process is that person to which the team makes their final recommendation. (A process owner is usually determined to be the person who receives the acclaim for the success of a process *or* receives the blame for its problems.)

The facilitator works with the chairperson to determine that the team develops a clear, concise, and focused mission statement or objective. Additionally, the facilitator assists in developing a schedule of meetings, reinforcing the need for attendance

127

at these meetings, and determining that the meetings have preplanned and communicated agendas. Additionally, the facilitator assists the chair in determining that minutes are taken at these meetings and distributed on a timely basis.

Clearly, it is *not* the role of the facilitator to perform any of the actual tasks involved in team mechanics. Rather, they serve the role of process expert and perform a preventative function to ensure that team mechanics items are in place in order to maximize team effectiveness and impact.

Meeting effectiveness

The facilitator assists the team by monitoring meeting conduct. This includes both the presence and use of team mechanics elements discussed above, but also the actual conduct of the meetings. Specifically, are the meetings started and completed on time, are agendas followed, does the team stay on the agenda topics, are action assignments given and carried out on schedule?

Quality Improvement

The facilitator serves as advisor to the team concerning the Quality Improvement process and its implications on the team. Specifically, the facilitator directs the team concerning the proper Quality Improvement process tools to consider in examining and solving their stated objective. Additionally, the facilitator assists in determining that the team is truly targeting for the elimination of problems and prevention versus 'quick fixes'.

Facilitators

Facilitators will make a major contribution to the success of the organization. They should *not* be seen as 'oracles' who have all the answers, but as facilitators who will make the process of developing the correct answer easier.

They should work well with others. They should have an open and creative mind. They should be direct enough to voice their opinions, but circumspect enough to know when to remain silent. They should be familiar with the proper conduct of teams and

128

meetings and the basics of the Quality Improvement process. (These last items can be developed. The initial qualities are not easily attained through training.)

RECOGNITION OF RESULTS

An important aspect of corrective action is the recognition of its success by management. Certainly, it is a fundamental principle of psychology that what gets rewarded gets repeated. It is true for our pets and it is also true for our organizations. Therefore, if we want corrective action to succeed and continue – to become part of our culture – then we must reward and recognize it as we do other vital elements in business, such as forecast attainment, profit targets, and cost improvement efforts.

Further, if we want to reinforce corrective action through teamwork, then we must recognize and reward teams that are successful. This entire subject of recognition will be covered in an upcoming chapter, but we touch on it here because it is an integral part of reinforcing corrective action.

This recognition need not be monetary. In fact, it is preferable that it is not monetary. We want effective corrective action to be a normal part of business, not an exception, so we really should not be paying people for 'doing their job'. However, we should recognize and celebrate their successes and publicize them to the organization.

Several organizations invited teams that had successfully completed corrective action projects to present their results to the management board. These presentations could be formal, with charts, graphs, and overheads, or informal with just bullet points on an easel pad. Some groups even presented 'skits' dramatizing the 'before' and 'after' of their corrective action projects. Of course, the key is not the presentation format, but the fact that corrective action is taking place, that senior management cares, and that management is recognizing these employees and communicating this recognition to the organization.

It may sound silly, but it is absolutely amazing what a 'thank you, nice job' from the 'top banana' can do towards making corrective action second nature in an organization. This is why recognition is such a key part of effective corrective action.

Because prevention is how we are going to be making Quality happen, we should practice prevention on the subject of corrective action and address a situation which will certainly arise when we begin to implement corrective action.

A team of employees identifies a problem and works together to solve it and eliminate its cause forever. The permanent elimination of this problem will save the organization X thousands of dollars or pounds. Do we 'cut' the employees in on the savings? If corrective action is going to be so effective and eliminate so many problems, and therefore save us so much money, shouldn't we share these savings with the employees taking the action that precipitated these savings?

Before jumping directly into a possible approach to this situation, let's review our objectives for Quality. First, we want this emphasis on Quality to become part of our organization's culture. We do not want Quality to be some sort of added appendage, something extraneous to the basic core nature of the organization. Secondly, we want Quality to serve as the focal point of our corporate culture's evolution from one of fire-fighting and trouble-shooting to one which practices prevention and is focused unswervingly on continuous improvement and our customers.

In light of these objectives, we should review our existing policy for rewarding employees for significant contributions. We may find that the organization already has a process for rewarding employees in such situations. Some organizations have 'special recognition bonuses' which are given to employees, or teams of employees, for just this type of success. Interestingly, the companies we studied rarely, if ever, disbursed the total amounts allocated and budgeted for these bonuses. This is just another example of what a poor job most corporate managements do in recognizing employee contributions.

Additionally, we want to be very careful that we do not set a precedent of rewarding employees for just 'doing their jobs'. The problem lies in the fact that management has historically done such a poor job of recognition that some effort is needed to raise employees' sights concerning activities and behavior which should be accepted and expected. Specifically, employees should begin to see that continuous improvement means that they should be constantly seeking ways to do their jobs better. That can mean shorter cycle times, cost improvements, cost avoidances, or entirely new processes.

Management should see it as their responsibility to continually reinforce this behavior through recognition. Further, those making significant contributions should be recognized by the entire organization, as we will discuss in Chapter 10. However, we should not get into the habit of paying off for each success, each contribution. One company even developed a sliding scale of monetary rewards – this type of improvement earned you £X, this type earned you £Y.

You can clearly see that this type of approach is going to lead to disgruntled employees – 'how come they got £X and we only got £Y?' It will also add further bureaucracy to the organization at a time when we are trying to eliminate it. Finally, it will clearly be seen by all employees as something added on to the culture, not something intrinsic to it.

Therefore, avoid the pay-off approach and concentrate on making real recognition an integral part of our corrective action process and our organization.

An organization that aggressively pursues the development of an effective corrective action process will stand in good stead with both the Baldrige and ISO 9000 standards. Corrective action is specifically addressed in both and in a very similar fashion. The Baldrige criteria directly address the subject of corrective action in Category five – Quality Assurance of Products and Services. This category in general, and items within it in particular, address the need to determine root causes of problem situations. Moreover, the ISO 9000 standards have two separate sections dealing with the related issues of non-conformity and its control (Section 14.0) and Corrective Action (Section 15.0). These sections go into great detail concerning the need for a systematic approach for identifying and eliminating problems forever. Importantly, both the Baldrige and ISO 9000 standards are consistent in their proactive and prevention-oriented approach to corrective action. Both are clear that Quality is prevention, not problem solving.

131

IMPLEMENTATION ACTION 5: SUMMARY

Let's review the key actions necessary to make effective correction action an integral part of our organization's culture.

1. Assign the responsibility for developing our customized corrective action process to a member of our management board.
2. Determine that whatever process is developed and approved by our Quality implementation team is included as part of our Quality training program.
3. Emphasize that our corrective action system concentrate on problem resolution and permanent elimination and *not* on the tracking, reporting, or cataloguing of corrective action projects.
4. Consider the use of a form as a vehicle for communicating the status or the facts involved in our corrective action projects. The form should be maintained by those doing the corrective action and should serve as a repository for their learning as they proceed with their corrective action project. Additionally, consider the use of 'facilitators' to accelerate and focus our corrective action projects.
5. Recognize the successful corrective action teams at all levels of the organization. Remember, 'what gets recognized gets repeated'. This recognition should come from the highest levels of our organization and should be shared with the entire organization.

Implementation action 6
Quality council

9

The Brontosaurus had two functional brains. One was located in its head, some 50 feet off the ground at times. The other brain was located at the base of its tail, somewhat closer to the action. The similarities between dinosaurs and many corporations are numerous, but the Brontosaurus has a distinct advantage with its two brains.

Most corporations are driven from the top. All the ideas, plans, and direction comes from a small group of managers. Employee participation, in general, is minimal and rarely solicited. This is in sharp contrast to many world-class corporations where employee participation is a vital component to generating new ideas, developing process improvements, and adding value while reducing costs.

This participatory style is often seen as a Japanese development. Yet, employee participation in Quality Improvement is not solely limited to the Far East. The Milliken Company has been implementing Quality Improvement for over nine years. They have stimulated their employees to the benefits of Quality and Continuous Improvement and, led by firm, unswerving management ownership of Quality, they have developed an organization that averages over 15 suggestions per year *per employee*. These suggestions are not the 'we ought to have more Mexican food in the cafeteria' variety. Rather, they are suggestions and ideas on improving Milliken's processes and thereby its competitive position in the industry.

Fifteen suggestions per employee per year may appear phenomenal to other organizations. They may be faced with a total of fifteen ideas from their entire management staff in a year! However, even

133

Milliken's impressive record is dwarfed by the organizations leading the Quality revolution. Most notable among these is Toyota, which averages over 50 suggestions per employee per year. That is an organization that understands competitiveness, the customer orientation of Quality Improvement, and the need for continuous improvement in order to remain competitive.

So how do we determine how well our Quality Improvement efforts are progressing if we are just starting the process? What if we have not yet established an employee participation level capable of generating significant input for improving our processes? And, given our substantial investment in time and talent in our Quality Improvement effort, how do we know if we are able to generate important returns and start the journey toward Quality Improvement?

This is the function of the Quality council. They are the 'eyes and ears' of the organization, particularly at the early stages of our Quality Improvement efforts. Their role is to convey to management the true state of the organization's efforts. In theory, management should understand where their organization is at any point in time. However, reality often finds management distant and not in close contact with the real state of the organization. Therefore, there is the need for this type of 'in-house' market research that can provide a clear indication of our progress, or lack thereof.

The Quality council comprises the thought leaders from throughout our organization. They should represent a clear cross-section of the organization, so that we can learn about the impact of our efforts on everyone. The Quality council will tell us what is reality versus what our perceptions might be. This function of the Quality council will identify what parts of our process need fine tuning and which are proceeding as planned. The Quality council is a preventative function which will keep the organization from making dramatic shifts or refinements in its process several years into the effort.

A case in point, one organization implementing Quality Improvement did not believe it needed a Quality council. This organization's management was confident that they would know the state of the organization without additional counsel. This management also spent a great deal of money on Quality implementation and particularly on celebratory events upon the conclusion of Quality training.

They confused 'conspicuous consumption' in the form of costly and showy celebrations with real management ownership of the basic concepts of Quality Improvement.

Moreover, this management never changed their basic management style to reflect the basic concepts of Quality Improvement and this was immediately perceived by the organization. Quality Improvement had become another 'program' which the organization saw as concluding upon the completion of the Quality training classes.

It was not until two years into the implementation of their Quality Improvement process that the management of this organization realized that a dramatic redirection was necessary. Quality was not happening and they could not understand why. Of course, no thought was ever given to re-examining management's habits and practices. Nor was any thought given to asking the customers about their needs and expectations concerning the organization's products and services. Rather, it was concluded that Quality was impractical for their particular industry, although major competitors were concurrently embarking on Quality Improvement efforts and achieving important results with a customer focused approach.

An effective Quality council would have provided immediate insight to this management, particularly concerning their behavior and its impact on the organization. Minor course changes could have been made along the way, instead of the drastic changes contemplated two years into implementation.

Our Quality council should be selected by the management board at the outset of our Quality Improvement implementation. Many organizations make a mistake by waiting until the implementation efforts are well underway before forming a Quality council. Better to form this group at the outset and have the benefit of their insight throughout the formative early stages of the process than wait until the plans are 'set in cement'.

The council should develop its own mission statement and get the approval of the management board on their needs and expectations. This mission statement would merely detail the 'scope' of the council's responsibilities. They should then meet on a monthly basis and review specific elements of the organization's implementation plan and also share the feedback obtained from within their areas of influence. It is important that the organization fully

135

Quality Council Charter

Charter Excerpts	What This Means in English
The PURPOSE of the Quality Council is to provide an objective means of monitoring Dental Care Company employee understanding of, commitment to, and implementation experience in our Quality Improvement Process (QIP).	Our goal is to improve the work environment and performance of Dental Care Company.
We communicate QIP issues, activities, concerns, successes and opportunities to the Quality Improvement Team (QIT) and specific subcommittees for their evaluation and further action.	Neither rain, nor sleet, nor gloom of night will stop us from delivering your messages and words of wisdom.
The Quality Council FUNCTIONS as a Subcommittee of the QIT.	We giveth—(our intent is to be an active advisor to the QIT).
The QIT may request the Quality Council to review specific matters and report its findings.	And we taketh—(we will work on assignments that we receive from the QIT).
The Council members OBTAIN INFORMATION about our QIP through interaction with employees and subcommittees (through receiving subcommittee minutes). Information obtained will drive Quality Council activities. Conclusions and recommendations will be communicated to the QIT.	We will talk to you in your office, in our offices, in the parking lot, over a cup of coffee, or while jogging at LIVE FOR LIFE®. We will pass on QIP problems, concerns and successes to the QIT. We will follow-up with the QIT to see what actions they are taking.
Quality Council members do not actively determine QIP actions to be taken. Specific subcommittee actions resulting from Quality Council recommendations will be communicated to employees by the appropriate subcommittees.	We are the Conduit! We are your voice to raising and resolving issues.
Our MEMBERSHIP consists of volunteer representatives of each division.	We are an all-around great bunch of guys and gals! We are interested and concerned with the QIP and are committed to implement change within Dental Care Company.
Rotation of members will occur from time to time.	Membership applications are always accepted!!
The Quality Council ORGANIZATION consists of a chairperson who coordinates the Quality Council activities. Responsibility for the minutes rotates among QC members. The Quality Council will meet initially biweekly and at a minimum monthly.	Our facilitator is Bruce Kohut. The Quality Council gang includes: Brad Cochran, Joan Gonzalez, Carol Harris, Fran Kleinbard, Bruce Kohut, Peg Levy, Mark New, and Lynn Morgan.

Figure 9.1 An example of how an organization addressed the issue of a Quality council – articles from the company newspaper.

Dental Care Company Quality Council

by Lynn Morgan

The purpose of the Quality Council is to keep the entire DCC Quality Improvement Process (QIP) on track. In essence, our goal is to improve our work environment and our performance as a Company which can only be accomplished through open communications. The Quality Council is committed to keeping the channels of communications open and our major responsibility includes serving as a liaison between our fellow employees and the QIP organization.

A Voice In Raising and Resolving Issues

Successful communication is a two-fold process and in order to meet our goals, the Quality Council needs to obtain information about QIP from our fellow employees—welcoming questions and concerns, as well as monitoring successes. For the Council, information is defined as anything involving the Quality Improvement Process—issues, activities, opportunities, suggestions and achievements. When an issue is raised about the Process, the Council's role is not to determine what action should be taken, but rather to assess the situation and pass the issue on to the Quality Improvement Team (QIT) or appropriate subcommittee. The Council then follows up to make sure that every issue has been handled and communicates the results back to employees.

A System For Gathering Information

We need to hear from you. Council members will have small "Quality Council" signs by their nameplates on the hallway wall outside their offices. So please stop in, call, or drop us a note with your thoughts on the Quality Improvement Process.

Fran Kleinbard
X-2136, J H-315

Peg Levy
X-2501, JH-526

Joan Gonzalez
X-3859, JH-511

Mark New
X-3483, JH-130

Carol Harris
X-3890, JH-317

Brad Cochran
X-3873, JH-510

Lynn Morgan
X-2114, JH-401

Bruce Kohut
X-1543, East Research 1211

The Council, chaired by Bruce Kohut of Research, consists of eight volunteers representing each DCC divisions. Our members will be profiled in upcoming issues of Quality Starts With Me. The Council meets twice a month and looks forward to your input to ensure our successful implementation of the Quality Improvement Process and our success as a Company.

What's Your Opinion

What do you see as the role of the Quality Council in the Quality Improvement Process?

"The Quality Council's role is to monitor QIP at Dental Care Company. We will bring employees' concerns and input to the Quality Council meetings for discussion and recommendation. The Council will then present this information to the Quality Improvement Team for their evaluation and further action. We will follow up with the Quality Improvement Team to see what actions they are taking."

—**Joan K. Gonzalez,**
Quality Council

"I see the role of the Quality Council as the 'sounding board' to the Q.I.T. We are responsible for conveying to the Q.I.T. how the QIP process is going in our Company through interaction with the employees and various subcommittees."

—**Brad Cochran,**
Quality Council

"The role of the Quality Council is to keep the Quality Improvement Process on track. We're committed to keeping communications flowing throughout the QIP organization and to our employees."

—**Lynn Morgan,**
Quality Council

"The purpose of the Quality Council is to monitor the progress of the Quality Improvement Process. Successes and deficiencies in the QIP can be identified and appropriate action taken. We are not the corrective action subcommittee which is involved with the day-to-day quality business issues. The QC is interested in the Quality process itself and the cultural change that is occurring at Dental Care. We need everyone's help. We want to talk with all Dental Care employees to hear their comments, ideas and suggestions on the QIP process. A true Quality culture at Dental Care can only happen with the full participation of all Dental Care employees."

—**Dr. Bruce Kohut,**
Quality Council

3

137

understand the purpose of the Quality council and recognize its constituents, as this group is a key sounding board for the entire organization.

The management board should receive input from the council through a copy of their meeting minutes, or possibly through direct follow-up meetings should the need arise. Importantly, any issues surfaced by the council should be addressed by the appropriate functional groups, or by the management board directly. The quality council should not be a corrective action group. Nor should it be seen as a group that must correct any of the issues it observes and reports on.

An example of how one organization addressed the issue of a Quality council is illustrated in Fig.9.1 in two articles appearing in the organization's newspaper on the subject of the Quality council.

The subject of a Quality council is too tactical an element in our Quality Improvement effort for either the Baldrige criteria or the ISO 9000 standards. The Baldrige criteria allude to the need for employee input into our Quality Improvement effort in Category 4.0 – Human Resource Utilization. Item 4.2 – Employee Involvement – specifically addresses the need for employee input into our process, so our Quality council is certainly consistent with the intent of the Baldrige criteria. Importantly, the need for a Quality council has become obvious based upon the 'lessons learned' of a wide variety of organizations. In our research we could not find one organization that had a Quality council – or similar group – that regretted taking this action. Conversely, we continually found organizations like the one mentioned earlier, who sincerely wished they had not tried to 'short-cut' this item and thereby miss an important opportunity for employee involvement and feedback.

IMPLEMENTATION ACTION 6: SUMMARY

Let's summarize the key implementation actions concerning a Quality council.

1. The management board as Quality implementation team should select a Quality council as part of its initial plan for implementing Quality Improvement.

2. The Quality council should comprise representatives from across our organization. Members should come from a variety of levels and disciplines. The key selection criteria for the council should be that its members are 'thought leaders' from their particular organization and are in close contact with, and can speak for, large parts of our organization.

3. The Quality council should meet and develop its own objectives, possibly putting these in the form of a mission statement. They should obtain approval to this set of objectives from the Quality implementation team.

4. The Quality council's members and the council's objectives should be communicated to the organization through our awareness effort and through the direct line management. The organization should feel free to share their thoughts and feelings with this group, and if need be, to surface issues with its members which they are unable to raise, or uncomfortable about presenting, to their own management.

5. The council should meet regularly and address specific and timely issues related to the implementation of our Quality process. They should also discuss their 'feedback' from their parts of the organization. They should copy the Quality implementation team on the minutes of their meetings and arrange special 'face to face' sessions should the need arise.

Implementation action 7 Communication

10

We have stated it earlier, but it bears repeating that the two key elements for Making Quality Happen are *prevention* and *communication*.

Prevention because it is no longer feasible in today's business environment to effectively react to competition. To succeed, you must innovate, lead, attack. *L'audace, toujours l'audace!* It is no longer sufficient to have excellent competitive information and intelligence. By the time we read or hear about patents, New Drug Applications (NDA's), or capital equipment purchases, it is already too late. Competitors are shrinking their cycle times to market for new products, new technologies, new services. Therefore, we must be proactive, we must practice prevention.

Communication is vital to Quality Improvement because the successful organization of the 1990s and beyond will be a tightly-knit team, functioning as one unit, not a series of separate units barely functioning, or worse, functioning at cross-purposes. Communication will break down the internal barriers within our organizations so that we can become more efficient and effective. Communication will guarantee that we are not repeating the same mistakes throughout our organization. Clearly, there is nothing wrong with mistakes unless we keep repeating them and fail to learn from them. We cannot learn, develop, and grow without mistakes.

Most importantly, communication with our customer is critical to real Quality Improvement. We must continually strive to communicate more effectively with our customers and understand why those who are currently not our customers have chosen that course.

141

We cannot learn these important lessons without effective and ongoing customer communication.

However, those organizations that communicate poorly are doomed to repeat mistakes which are not communicated throughout the organization due to a false sense of pride, fear, or a fiefdom mentality. Moreover, they will be so internally focused that they will neither seek out their customers nor seek to learn from them.

In our discussion of determining clear customer needs and expectations for our goods and services, we detailed the importance of effective communication with our customers and suppliers. We also stressed the need to be outwardly focused – what's going on in the world around our organization – so that we may more effectively compete and succeed in that arena.

However, we cannot forget the great importance of effectively communicating within our organization. This effective internal communication is the driving force behind our Quality Improvement efforts. It is so vital to our success that we have developed two related, yet separate, actions to address this issue. These two implementation actions are *awareness* and *recognition*. Taken together as communication, they are the fuel that drives our Quality Improvement engine.

AWARENESS

Awareness is the first part of our communications effort. A successful awareness effort is critical if our Quality Improvement initiative is to grow and prosper. Our awareness program must span our entire Quality undertaking. At its outset, our organization must understand the 'why, what and how' of Quality, just as this book explained them to you. The organization needs to know our goals, objectives, strategies, and tactics. They need to know the timing of our efforts, and most importantly, they need to know how it will all impact them. Then they will need to be continually informed concerning the current status of our efforts and the successes we have achieved.

Failure to provide this information creates a communications void which the employees will immediately fill by 'creating' the required information. Anyone familiar with any organization knows that the strength and credibility of an organization's 'rumor hot-line' is inversely proportional to the amount of information provided the organization by management. Therefore, we cannot allow our Quality initiative to founder, or be subject to the whims of an organization, for lack of clear, consistent communication. Our Quality process represents far too great an investment in time and talent to risk its failure due to our 'failure to communicate', in the immortal words of 'Cool Hand' Luke.

Directly related to the need to communicate effectively within our organization is the need to communicate positively. Success breeds success, and it is never more evident than in Quality. Nationally, how do we know who the successful companies in Quality Improvement are? They are the ones who tell us they're successful. The Toyotas, Philips, Millikens, Federal Expresses, Xeroxes, and Motorolas have all effectively publicized their efforts and their successes. One of the important features of the American National Quality Award named for the late Commerce Secretary Malcolm Baldrige is the awareness component it represents. The winners of this award, and Japan's even more prestigious Deming Prize, become the font of all quality knowledge. Their status within industry is elevated even beyond its deserved high status in the business pantheon.

Accentuate the positive. Within a major Fortune 50 organization one division was achieving very positive results with its Quality Improvement efforts. How do we know? Well, they took every opportunity to tell anyone who would listen about their successes. Any problems? Almost certainly, but you never heard about those problems from this division.

Conversely, other divisions would meet to discuss their Quality efforts and trade 'problem' stories. This negative news reinforced basic doubts and the daunting challenge posed by the cultural change of Quality Improvement. Pretty soon, what started as a challenging matter had become an insurmountable one, merely based upon the nature of communications exchanged between divisions. Again, the power of positive thinking cannot be underestimated. Effective leaders make their organizations believe that even the greatest obstacles can be overcome. Ineffective leaders will allow their organizations to stumble over the slightest hurdle.

Our awareness effort must precede the actual start of our Quality Improvement process. It is particularly important that in the initial phases of our process we communicate almost continually with our organization. Importantly, this communication should use the full scope of media available to us, but with a particular emphasis on face to face, manager to employee discussions that are too often missing from our organizations. If such manager–employee meetings are not now an integral part of our organization's culture, then the Quality Improvement effort can provide an ideal opportunity for initiating this important communication vehicle.

The initial awareness event should be a presentation by management to employees in which the 'why, what, and how' of our Quality Improvement effort are explained. Explained rather than detailed. The organization is interested in the basic fundamentals initially, with a major emphasis on how our proposal will impact their job, their way of working, their world. This initial presentation is best done with the entire organization at one time. That way, everyone hears the same message. No gaps, no rumors. However, the size of many organizations precludes this scenario. In that case, a series of presentations should be scheduled and tightly scheduled at that.

It is vitally important to cover all employees, with an emphasis on *all*. One large organization with numerous factories scheduled a management road show in which the company president spoke with all factory workers – first, second, and third shifts. That's Management Ownership and that sends a valuable message at the onset of the process. Importantly, this type of face to face encounter, on the employees 'pitch' if possible, has far greater positive impact than even the slickest promotional piece or audio-visual '*son et lumière*' show, and does so far more efficiently.

This efficiency message is not lost on employees. Management many times undermines their most well-intentioned efforts on the subject of efficiency and productivity by turning the presentation into a glitzy audio-visual event to create impact. Organizations quickly learn what these events cost and the message on efficiency or productivity is immediately swamped by the cost of presenting it.

These face to face sessions should become the cornerstone of our awareness effort. They should be conducted every six months, ideally every quarter. The topic of each need not always be solely dedicated

144

to Quality, but we should use these opportunities to continually update the organization on the status of our process, its latest successes, and how these successes have beneficially impacted our organization.

An important follow-up to the introductory sessions can be a written description of the Quality process. Most organizations have a newspaper, newsletter, or some form of written communications vehicle. That vehicle should now become an integral part of our awareness process. It is important that existing communications vehicles be used in our awareness effort. We should not seek to create entirely new ones just for our Quality process. For example, do not create a Quality newsletter or newspaper. Use existing media. This is important because we want Quality and Quality Improvement to be part of our normal organization, not something added on or tangential to the organization. However, we may want to expand our current vehicles and have an entire page or column devoted to Quality.

Our discussion on Quality at this early juncture should provide the organization with the relevant details it desires. Who will form the Quality implementation team, who will serve on and chair the various other *ad-hoc* committees? Will everyone serve on committees, or will just a few people be called upon, on an *ad-hoc* basis? What are the functions of the committees and are they permanent or temporary? What training will all employees receive about Quality, when will it start, who will be the instructors, how long will it last?

These are just some of the questions our organization is going to want answered early on in our implementation of Quality Improvement. Therefore, an awareness committee should be formed. This will be one of the few 'permanent' committees in our process. The awareness committee's role is to share information about the implementation of our Quality Improvement efforts with the entire organization. Therefore, the members of this committee ideally should be those within the organization who have some real experience in effective communication, such as sales or marketing, for example.

An important first step for this awareness committee is to develop a calendar of communication-awareness events. This calendar is really a marketing plan for our awareness effort. It should detail the information we want communicated and the media by which it will be presented to the organization.

For example, an important medium we want as a permanent part of our new Quality culture is a quarterly, or semi-annual, communications meeting. It should be chaired by our chief executive and attended by all employees. The awareness committee should develop a list of topics related to our Quality efforts that they want communicated at each of these sessions.

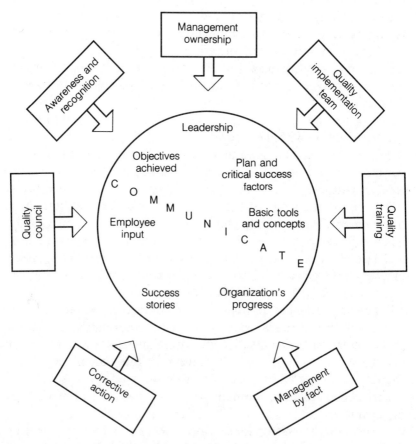

Figure 10.1 The essential communication process between the various Quality committees and teams, via the awareness committee.

Additionally, the awareness committee should work with our company newspaper–newsletter editor and develop an entire awareness schedule for this vehicle. This schedule should cover topics to be presented and also who will be responsible for producing the article. The awareness committee will become 'cub reporters' initially – producing many of the early articles about our Quality process. However, their goal should be to include as many other employees as possible in the writing of these articles – particularly the 'success stories'. Again, the organization needs to be informed that we want to hear about their successes, no matter of what size or from what level within the organization.

Also, the awareness committee must inform all other elements of our Quality Improvement effort that it is vital to share information concerning the various aspects of our process. For example, when the education committee has developed a Quality training curriculum and training schedule, this information should be communicated to the entire organization through our awareness vehicles. In fact, it is vital to the initial success of our Quality efforts that all committees, or Quality related teams, share their information with our awareness committee.

The awareness committee should not assume the long-term role of reporters searching out the news of Quality Improvement. After the initial Quality launch period, the various Quality committees and teams should assume the role of 'stringers' and report their news, status, and success to the awareness committee, who will then disseminate this information to the organization through the appropriate media (Fig 10.1).

COMMUNICATION OPPORTUNITIES

It is important to consider all communications vehicles available to an organization when developing our awareness program. Not every organization will have access to all the different types of communications we will discuss, but we should consider all those which are a normal part of our current operation. Again, it is important to remember that our awareness effort must be a normal and natural part of our culture, not something 'force fit' or extraneous. Remember, we want Quality to be part of a new culture for our organization, not something external to it.

147

Here are some examples of communications vehicles, besides newspapers and company meetings, which numerous organizations have implemented as part of their Quality Improvement efforts.

Bulletin boards

These are an important and integral part of the communications plan in many organizations. Bulletin boards are used by a variety of firms as the major source of employee information and therefore are particularly important when developing our Quality related communications plan. Such bulletin boards are invariably centrally located – possibly near the cafeteria or break rooms – and may contain certain job postings and important announcements, even notices of items employees wish to sell. They are an ideal source for conveying Quality information to employees because they already are an important source of other 'news of value' to our fellow employees. One organization heightened the emphasis on Quality in all its bulletin boards by framing them in a large wooden 'Q'.

As with all communications vehicles, it is important to frequently update the information appearing on such boards. They are important communication vehicles because they present information that is timely and relevant to employees. Therefore, update the information presented on a regular and frequent basis. Have 'success stories' ready to post each month. Nothing is worse than seeing the same notice for an extended period of time. When this occurs, employees will pay less and less attention to these boards and we will lose a valuable communication vehicle.

Newsletters

For the sake of this discussion, newsletters are defined as one sheet, two sided notices usually developed and reproduced in-house. They are frequently the main communication vehicle in smaller organizations. With the space limitations imposed by the newsletter format, it is critical to make certain that the information communicated is clear, concise, and to the point.

Additionally, newsletters may serve a summarizing role following a major communications event such as the recommended quarterly

148

employee meetings with our chief executive. Clearly, if our organization is small and has a newsletter in place of a newspaper, then it is also small enough to have the chief executive address the employees on a face to face basis, and to do so frequently.

We may want to consider increasing the frequency of the newsletter – monthly is ideal – if we consistently have too much information and too little space. Varying the color of the paper stock used for the newsletter will alert employees to new editions and increase readership. Active readership is very important for both newsletters and our newspapers, as we expend a great deal of effort producing these vehicles and therefore we should do everything possible to maximize readership and content recall.

Posters

Posters have always been an important communications medium. We have all seen, and can easily visualize the famous James Montgomery Flagg 'Uncle Sam' recruiting poster. Posters can also play an important role in our Quality awareness effort, for as Flagg was trying to do with his recruiting posters, we are also trying to enlist the spirit and enthusiasm of our organization for the cultural changes of Quality Improvement.

Posters are extremely impactful in that they communicate the desired message quickly and directly. Often they do so with humor or irony. It is now possible to subscribe to poster services that can provide posters for our organization on a variety of themes – Quality among them. While these can be helpful and are certainly entertaining, they can be viewed by our employees as something external to the organization. In fact, the organization's perception is correct – the posters are developed and distributed by an outside service and we are usually forced to mold the posters to our needs. Many times this force-fit is painfully evident.

Better to develop our own posters to match our organization's personality and meet the needs of our Quality Improvement effort. Additionally, these internally developed posters provide a further way to involve others within our organization, particularly those with creative and artistic inclinations.

One organization which has experienced great success in implementing Quality Improvement has a graphic artist on their staff and he produced an outstanding series of posters on a Quality Improvement theme. Many of the posters featured the likenesses of fellow employees – nothing could be more internal to an organization than that! These posters were rotated throughout the headquarters and manufacturing facility, so they never became 'stale' or 'old news'. This is particularly important with posters, as they are best employed for impact and as a reminder of our quest for Quality.

Another organization combined awareness with our next action, recognition, in their use of posters. They used poster size photographs of employees, or teams of employees, who had made important contributions to the organization's Quality efforts, such as serving as a Quality training instructor or taking part on a successful corrective action team. These color posters were placed in the company's cafeteria with an explanation of the team's or individual's accomplishments relating to Quality.

Each month a new series of individual or team portraits was placed in the cafeteria and the previous month's were given to the employees to take home. You can imagine how having your portrait, or your team's picture, posted publicly can both reinforce and remind employees about Quality. It can also make them aware of the successes being achieved by their fellow employees.

Department meetings

Many times employees will feel overwhelmed at the start of Quality Improvement efforts because the problems facing our organization may seem insurmountable. The large, highly visible problems invariably cross numerous functional areas and can involve a multitude of employees, supervisors, and managers. Where to begin?

Better to consider the Japanese expression that 'the whale is not eaten with one bite'. Therefore, we should not become engulfed by our organization's major problems, but rather concentrate on the problems confronting our specific part of that organization. That way, we can build from a series of small victories, small successes, and progress with continuous improvement, rather than trying to hit a 'home run' our first time at bat.

Department meetings can play an important role in personalizing our efforts to each employee. Additionally, they involve our peers

150

and develop the synergistic effects so important to successful team performance, and after all, what is our department – or our company for that matter – but a team? Department meetings also establish and develop the pivotal employee-supervisor relationship.

Quality Improvement will never be successful within our organization unless we have effective and constant two-way communication between employees and their supervisors, no matter at what level of the organization.

Examine the companies that have successfully implemented Quality Improvement and we invariably find excellent communication between employees and their supervisors throughout the organization. Also, we find that these successful organizations *work* at communicating, it does not 'just happen'.

Department meetings are an important part of this communication and awareness process. Not meetings for the sake of meetings, but brief, open, planned discussions where topics are presented, discussed, and closure reached or appropriate next steps agreed upon.

Initially, these department meetings can provide Management with an opportunity to present their views, goals, and objectives concerning our Quality Improvement effort. These meetings provide a natural setting for addressing specific questions employees may have, and these questions are more likely to surface in this type of environment than in the larger organization orientation sessions.

However, longer term these meetings can serve as the focus for our corrective action efforts and establish our attitude of continuous improvement. Employees should be encouraged to surface ideas for improving our processes, for increasing our effectiveness and efficiency. Their thoughts and commitment will stimulate creative thoughts and increased commitment on the part of their fellow employees and further the Quality Improvement efforts in our department. This will enable us to start to address our difficulties and problem processes, thereby producing the small successes and victories so critical at the outset of any major cultural change.

Department meetings should be formal *and* informal. Formal in that they are scheduled, this schedule communicated to the department's employees, and all employees attend. Formal in that these meetings have agendas and that they start and end on schedule. Informal in that employees should feel free to participate, to contribute, to forward

151

an idea, a suggestion, a concern. Informal in that status, or rank, within the organization should be totally de-emphasized. In such meetings we are all just employees trying to do the job better.

Importantly, we should not have a meeting just to have a meeting. There is a great 'meetings as Mount Everest' mentality in business today – we hold meetings because they're there. Rather, we should plan on a one hour meeting once a month with our department. Have a topic for the meeting. Develop, produce, and distribute an agenda before the meeting to all department members. This allows them time to put their thoughts together before they walk into the meeting. These meetings are also an opportunity to have someone in our department other than the manager act as a facilitator. This will not only utilize their skills as a facilitator, but will also promote discussion by having someone except the 'chief' direct the meeting.

Clearly, making meetings work for us, and not vice versa, will require some effort on our parts at the outset. However, we will soon find that effective meetings, like effective communications, can become a way of life in our organization if we plan and follow through.

We have touched on a few tactical elements in a communications plan. Certainly, this is not an all-inclusive list, but rather a sampling of the most frequently used vehicles. Communications is an action that should be directed by our most creative and responsive employees. They should be in touch with not only the other groups developing parts of our implementation plan – such as Quality training and corrective action – but also with the entire organization, through our Quality Council. Communications forms the heart of our Quality Improvement process. In Quality, as in life, we must continually work to keep that heart strong and constantly working.

RECOGNITION

One part of the orientation on Quality Improvement that we have given to over two thousand managers worldwide focuses on the subject of recognition. We ask the orientation attendees to take a few minutes and recall the most impactful and memorable recognition they have received in their business lives. We then ask for volunteers to share these recognition moments with the rest of the group.

Shockingly, but not surprisingly, the vast majority are unable to remember any truly special recognition. Others recall congratulatory letters from senior executives, receptions in their honor, luncheons, etc. A tiny minority mention financial rewards as having any lasting impact.

This brief introduction on recognition serves two purposes for those attending the orientation, and for those reading this book as well. First, it illustrates what a universally poor job we do at recognizing employee contributions, particularly the contributions of employees in the non-sales and research areas. These two groups invariably have the highest level of recognition programs. Secondly, it demonstrates the real impact that a sincere 'thank you, job well done' can have on employees, especially when compared with the prevalent management perception that only financial rewards are effective incentives.

Successful organizations know the value of effective recognition. The Milliken Company, recognized by Tom Peters as the 'best managed company in America' and winner of the 1989 Malcolm Baldrige Quality Award, places extraordinary emphasis on recognition as part of their Quality Improvement efforts. In fact, Milliken refers to corrective action as the 'engine of Quality Improvement' and recognition as the 'fuel' for that engine. This is absolutely correct and cannot be underestimated by any organization interested in effectively implementing the cultural change required for Quality Improvement.

Quite simply, recognition reinforces management's real ownership of Quality, and anything else within their organization. What gets recognized gets done. What is recognized and rewarded gets repeated.

We train animals by rewarding them when they perform the behavior we want. The same is true with our organization, though we are many times less conscious of it. However, if we are less aware of what we recognize and reward, and what message this transmits to the organization, the organization is not. Most organizations do so little recognition that the traditional promotions and job enhancements are the only recognition visible to the entire organization. Therefore, when organizations promote those who have achieved temporary, or even illusory results based upon short-term

153

planning, then the entire organization will begin to fall in line and become short-term oriented.

Moreover, if our organization places little or no emphasis on recognizing employee contributions and achievements, then that behavior will perpetuate itself throughout the organization. This behavior reached its low point in one organization we visited where it was explained that the 'absence of criticism is to be seen as adequate recognition'. Is there any wonder that industry is in such a sorry state when senior managers hold such beliefs and actually manage this way?

An effective recognition program must become an integral part of our organization's new culutre. It must become a normal part of our business life. This will require work at first, particularly if we are currently doing little or nothing to recognize employee contributions. However, there should be a logical tie to our Recognition program with our standard practices so that it is viewed by employees as possibly new, but consistent and a normal part of our organization.

START WITH MEASURABLE GOALS

Specifically, each unit within our organization should have goals on which they are measured. This is a normal part of our management practice, or at least should be. Clearly, if our departments do not have measurable goals and objectives, how are we able to evaluate the management and organizations they supervise?

Shockingly, many parts of our organization may not have measurable, quantifiable objectives, and therefore their evaluations are based upon subjective criteria – the 'warm and fuzzy' feelings of their supervisors. This invariably leads to inequities in evaluation and promotion. These issues are then reflected throughout the organization by disgruntled employees.

Additionally, the organization understands that evaluations are being done based upon qualitative criteria and therefore we are soon involved in the 'it's who you know not what you do' culture. This is certainly not the type of corporate culture that is going to lead us into a new era of productivity and Quality. In fact, it is exactly this type of corporate culture that will become extinct in the coming age of corporate commitment to Quality and the customer.

If each of our units has measurable goals for the year, these goals should be communicated to their entire organization. The organization's efforts should be focused on these goals and visible measurement should continually remind employees where the department stands concerning its objective. Our recognition efforts should reinforce these objectives – they should be an integral part of our overall goals and objectives, not something separate from them.

For example, let's look at a sales organization, probably the one part of most organizations which has at least some level of recognition. Our sales organization has clear, quantifiable objectives for the year. These can include both an overall monetary and unit sales level, but possibly also include distribution levels, successful call completion rates, facings of our products at retail, and new distributions obtained for our products. These overall goals are translated down throughout the sales organization so that everyone knows what is expected of them. There is *focus*.

Recognition is provided to those who exceed their objectives, who develop new ways of surpassing their objectives, and/or who make major new contributions to the performance of the entire organization. Anyone who has ever witnessed a sales award ceremony cannot help but be impressed by the enthusiasm generated and the commitment reinforcement this enthusiasm develops.

Certainly, much of the award system in a sales organization is based upon money – bonuses based upon percentage above sales quota. However, almost every salesperson we have interviewed has stated categorically that the greatest incentive to them is the recognition provided by the non-monetary award, such as Salesperson of the Year, President's Club, or Ring Club. These special forms of recognition are reserved for the very top sales performers and invariably include presentations in front of all their peers and some unique designation – special blazer, ring, and/or trophy – which is highly visible and which clearly sets the recipient apart from their fellow sales professionals.

What our recognition system must do is bring that same level of enthusiasm, excitement, and commitment which we found in the sales recognition system into the entire organization. Additionally, we

155

must tailor the recognition system to accomplish the organizational goals which we believe are most important, such as the development of teamwork. Therefore, our recognition system must be designed to reinforce and recognize teamwork, not the 'lone eagle' school of management. Remember, what gets recognized gets done. We want teamwork, then we must recognize teams that have accomplished important goals.

Additionally, recognition should be open to all parts of the organization and should have many winners versus just one. Too often management believes that too many winners dilutes the effort. This is only the case if the winners are being recognized for activities which really do not merit recognition. If you are fortunate to have an organization that is really performing and achieving the goals which you have set for it, then do not hesitate to provide the required recognition.

ONE APPROACH TO RECOGNITION

Let's examine the recognition system developed by one of our surveyed organizations. Clearly, this example, like all the others we have discussed, is only one example of how we can implement recognition.

The organization under discussion decided that it wanted to build a culture where teamwork was of paramount importance. Too often this organization had found that parts of the organization were really working at cross purposes, and so teamwork – and the elimination of functional barriers – was the organization's objective. Therefore, only teams were going to be recognized. The criteria for recognition were developed accordingly. Specifically, managers and supervisors would recommend teams in their areas of responsibility for recognition. Teams would be recognized when they had made a significant contribution to the success of the organization in regards to the objectives developed as part of the group's annual business plan. Additionally, recognition was also given to those who made other significant contributions, such as major cost savings, new process improvements, and/or major problem elimination.

156

Recognition for the first level of performance took the form of an attractive desk piece of stone with the company's emblem and motto inscribed. This desk piece also included the recipient's name, their team, and the motto for the recognition process – in this case, 'You are the Cornerstone to our Success' – hence the stone award. These were awarded to any team recommended by their supervisors. There was no judging of the team's accomplishments by some board or committee. The supervisors were deemed to be closest to the site of the success and therefore the management trusted them with selecting those worthy of recognition. Again, we see a not too subtle message being sent here through the recognition efforts – this is your company, our company, not just 'management's company'.

A second level of recognition was developed within this organization as well. This higher level would include for consideration all those who had received the initial recognition. They would now be eligible for the second award consideration. All recipients were reviewed at the end of the year and the management board then selected those who had made the most significant contribution to the success of the entire organization. Importantly, the management board did not concentrate only on those teams which had the greatest financial accomplishments, but rather on those which had really 'made a difference' in the organization.

These employees, as part of their teams, were recognized in front of their peers at the organization's annual dinner – or company meeting – and brought up in front of the entire group. Then a spokesperson from the team, or the entire team, presented what they had accomplished. In some instances, this took the form of a business presentation with overheads or slides, diagrams, etc. In other instances, teams actually acted out the problems they had addressed and corrected. Most importantly, it provided these employees with a 'moment in the sun' in front of their peers and made them feel very special. While there was no monetary award as part of this second level of recognition, each team member was provided with a small gift catalogue from which they could choose a modest gift.

Additionally, the organization had developed a plaque to honor each year's recipients of the grand award and this plaque was prominently displayed in a public area. An important part of this plaque was a picture of the winning team(s) for that year and a permanent listing of previous years' winners. They were not to be forgotten by the organization. Finally, the annual winners were honorary judges for future candidates for this award, so the employees were brought into the selection and recognition process. This makes it even more a part of the normal and natural way our organization works.

Let's summarize the benefits of this recognition system. It is tied to and reinforces our organization's business goals and objectives. The initial level of recognition is provided by the manager or supervisor, so that the organization's management structure is reinforced, not circumvented. The recognition is open to all and focuses on behavior the organization wants to reinforce, in this case teamwork. The awards chosen for the initial level were small, yet visible when placed in the employee's home or work area.

The second level of recognition was open to all employees in that it was selected from those who had been chosen for the initial recognition. The final selection was conducted by the management board with the input of the previous year's winners. This reinforces the fact that this recognition is an integral part of the organization – it is not being given out solely to management's 'pets'. The previous year's winners will make sure of that. Additionally, even at this level the awards are not ostentatious. Rather, they are something which the employees choose for themselves.

Finally, the recipients are publicly saluted by the organization, in front of their peers and management. This sends a direct and unmistakable message to the entire organization concerning the type of behavior management believes is most important. The recipients are also recognized permanently by having their team listed on a prominently displayed plaque which continually reminds them, and their peers, of their accomplishments. This further serves to encourage them to repeat this effort so that they might be placed on the plaque again. It also serves to encourage their fellow employees to strive for this honor and recognition.

Importantly, there is nothing 'hokey' or artificial about any of this. No one is being recognized because it is 'their turn'. The emphasis is on accomplishments – making things happen – and the behavior through which these things are made to happen – teamwork.

The entire recognition system is seen by all employees as an integral part of the organization because it is.

LINK AWARENESS AND RECOGNITION

The reason why the awareness and recognition actions are linked should now be evident. It is most important that our entire organization know exactly who is being recognized and why. Under our current systems the organization sees various people moving ahead, many times with a dramatically different 'public persona' than senior management sees. Therefore, it is vitally important to recognize the behaviors we want to be a central part of our new culture and to publicize that recognition throughout our entire organization. By doing so we reinforce the behaviors we desire.

This recognition should be publicized through organization-wide meetings, where the actual awards are presented, as we have already discussed. Additionally, our printed media, whether newspapers, newsletters, or bulletin boards, should certainly highlight these events for all employees to see. One major organization even has a quarterly video which is internally produced and distributed to all parts of the organization – even overseas units. What an ideal vehicle for disseminating our recognition information. Again, we should look at the media which are already part of our culture and utilize them to their fullest.

Both the ISO 9000 standards and the Baldrige National Quality Award criteria address the need for communication and both cover the topics of awareness and recognition. However, they do so in dramatically different levels of degree. In the ISO 9000 standards the issues of awareness and recognition merit a mention, but because these standards are really focused on a Quality control system, these two items are important, but clearly of a lesser priority.

Conversely, the Baldrige criteria are very demanding concerning the approach taken to both awareness and recognition. These two topics are covered extensively in the Human Resources Utilization category, which is the third largest in total point potential at 150 possible points, after Customer Satisfaction (300 possible points) and Quality Results (180 possible points.) Importantly, an organization approaching world class levels of performance would need to demonstrate their recognition results and levels via quantifiable data and trends over three or more years. Moreover, they would need to demonstrate that their Recognition approach reinforced their customer-focused objectives and that they continually evaluated their recognition approach for improvement. Quite clearly, the Baldrige criteria demonstrate that 'what gets recognized gets repeated'!

IMPLEMENTATION ACTION 7: SUMMARY

Let's summarize the awareness and recognition actions and highlight some key actions which should be considered for implementation.

Awareness

1. Review current awareness vehicles – newspapers, newsletters, bulletin boards, company meetings, department meetings. Determine exactly how our organization currently shares information and plan to utilize these vehicles and consider adding others, particularly face-to-face management–employee meetings.
2. Develop a listing of the subjects which we want communicated to the organization. Included within this list should be a discussion of the 'why, what, and how' of our Quality Improvement effort.
3. Develop a media plan for awareness in which the subjects we want communicated and the vehicles which can be used to communicate this information are combined.
4. Assign employees to develop the articles which will be included in our various media.
5. Inform the various other committee chairpeople and the Quality council that the awareness committee should be made aware of any and all activities of these other groups.

Recognition

1. Examine the current recognition program in our organization. Plan to either expand this program to include all employees or develop an entirely new one which includes all employees.
2. Develop the criteria by which employees, or preferably teams of employees, will be recognized. Gain the input of our managers and supervisors, so that they are part of the program and are committed to it from the outset.
3. Develop the actual mechanics of the recognition program. This includes the various levels of recognition and the awards which will accompany each level.
4. Share the detail of the plan with the awareness committee so that they can share it with the entire organization.
5. Monitor the results of both the awareness and recognition programs through the Quality council and obtain their input and recommendations concerning changes, if and when such changes are necessary.

11

What does a quality organization look like? – the Malcolm Baldrige National Quality Award, winning isn't everything!

If we are going to proceed with our Quality Improvement effort, how will we know if we are making any headway? Clearly, we are making a substantial investment of our organization's time and effort, so how are we going to know if we are starting to recoup this investment? Quite simply, what does an organization on the road to making Quality happen look like?

A variety of guideposts have been developed to assist us on this journey, including the American Malcolm Baldrige National Quality Award criteria, the ISO 9000 standards, and the guidelines for Japan's Deming Prize. However, while the Deming Prize guidelines and the ISO 9000 standards provide exceptionally useful insight for evaluating our Quality Improvement effort, the Baldrige Award criteria cover the broadest Quality spectrum. The far-reaching nature of these criteria reflects the fact that the Baldrige Award is the newest of these three Quality standards and thus has been able to build upon the experiences of its two predecessors. Similarly, we can also profit by utilizing the Baldrige criteria for our organization's benefit.

By way of background, the Malcolm Baldrige National Quality Award has three basic objectives. First, it seeks to create and build awareness of the importance of Quality and Quality Improvement as a competitive advantage in American organizations, public and private, profit and non-profit, manufacturing and service, large and small. Importantly, whether our organization is in Washington or Warsaw, the Baldrige criteria are relevant as standards of world-class performance. Because the award happens to be an American award for American organizations does not mean that international organizations cannot benefit from a complete knowledge of its criteria.

Secondly, the award was created to recognize those organizations that are excelling in the achievement and management of Quality and Quality Improvement. Thirdly, the award endeavors to promote a sharing of information concerning Quality and Quality Improvement implementation tools, techniques, and strategies.

But if we are just getting started in Quality Improvement, what does this National Quality Award have to offer us? We are probably years away from even considering application for any type of Quality award!

In fact, the real benefit to be gained by any organization from the Malcolm Baldrige National Quality Award is the use of the award's criteria to analyze and self-assess our organization. In reality, our objective should not be to win awards. We want to win in the marketplace. Therefore, our goal should be to achieve our organization's objectives by continuously improving the organization and better serving our customers and employees. We can measure our progress in this regard through a self-assessment versus the Baldrige Award criteria. These criteria provide an expanded 'ideal height and weight' chart for an organization, with categories on blood pressure, cholesterol, and exercise thrown in, to continue the analogy.

Just as we are well advised to regularly determine the state of our own physical well-being through a medical exam, so our organization will be well served by conducting a self-assessment based upon the Baldrige Award criteria. This self-assessment can be undertaken at any point along our Quality journey. In fact, a self-assessment can form the basis of an organization's initial introduction to the subject of Quality Improvement, as discussed in Chapter 3. An organizational self-assessment need not be overly rigorous at the outset, nor need it cover all seven Baldrige Award categories. In fact, an initial self-assessment utilizing the Leadership and Customer Satisfaction categories – representing 390 possible points out of a total potential of 1000 – is usually sufficiently illuminating, and distressing, to coalesce most management teams into action.

The Baldrige Award criteria are divided into seven categories totalling 1000 points. The categories and their respective point values are outlined below.

1.0 Leadership (90 points)
2.0 Information and Analysis (80 points)
3.0 Strategic Quality Planning (60 points)
4.0 Human Resource Management (150 points)
5.0 Management of Process Quality (140 points)
6.0 Quality and Operational Results (180 points)
7.0 Customer Focus and Satisfaction (300 points)

An excellent reference on the Malcolm Baldrige National Quality Award, its criteria, and an approach for applying for the actual award is Mark Graham Brown's thorough book, *Baldrige Award Winning Quality*. This book provides an easily understood application of the criteria and is an invaluable resource when considering an organizational self-assessment. Additionally, David A. Garvin of the Harvard Business School has written an excellent explanation of the real benefits to be gained from a thorough understanding of the Baldrige Award criteria. Professor Garvin's article, 'How the Baldrige Award Really Works', appeared in the *Harvard Business Review*, November–December, 1991, pp. 80–93. Our objective is not to cover that same ground, but to describe how the Baldrige Award criteria can be used as an important vehicle for facilitating our Quality Improvement journey.

It is important to understand that the Baldrige Award criteria do not tell organizations 'what' we should do in each of these areas – the criteria are not 'prescriptive' in nature. Rather, the criteria ask 'what are we doing' in each of these areas, thereby serving as a 'diagnostic' tool. However, our clear objective in making Quality happen is to learn from the previous lessons of other organizations implementing Quality Improvement and not to reinvent the wheel. Therefore our approach is slightly prescriptive to provide clear direction on how to implement a Quality Improvement effort and avoid the common pitfalls in order to assist organizations starting on what can otherwise be a daunting and difficult path.

It is therefore critically important that we always tailor our Quality implementation to our specific organization and conduct a self-assessment of that organization utilizing the Baldrige Award criteria to identify and learn about our strengths and areas for improvement. Based upon this self-assessment, we can then further develop and continuously improve our tailored Quality implementation plan.

When self-assessing our organization against the Baldrige Award criteria, it is important to consider the three part scoring system utilized in the award. This scoring system examines an organization's approach, deployment, and results. Let's take a brief look at what is meant by each of these.

Approach examines 'what' is actually being done in our organization regarding Quality and Quality Improvement. Importantly, the 'whats' that represent vital parts of a successful approach are exactly those we have addressed in this book. For example, is our organization customer focused and proactive, are we prevention oriented, are we driven by an attitude of continuous improvement, do we really have a Quality Improvement plan and do we continuously evaluate both our progress against that plan and also the plan itself? This can be seen in the human resources-training area, have we completed a training needs assessment for our organization? Have we developed an organization-wide training plan based upon that assessment, and are we continually evaluating both our training programs and our training planning process? This is an example of an approach to the subject of training.

It is most important to have a plan for implementing Quality Improvement. The Baldrige criteria challenge an organization to successfully execute a Quality Improvement plan, not to merely achieve success through a series of random marketplace wins and organizational pockets of success. Many organizations are successful in spite of themselves and an accurate self-asessment will identify these situations.

Deployment very simply examines how broadly our approach – our plan – is deployed throughout the organization and beyond. Is Quality just a manufacturing 'project' or is the whole organization involved? Does Quality Improvement extend to our products and services, our internal employees as well as our external customers and suppliers? And are we taking a public role in disseminating information about Quality Improvement to our communities and beyond? In our training example, have we completed a training needs assessment for our entire organization or just in the human resources and finance areas? This is a question of deployment – is our action evident throughout the organization or only in selected 'pockets'?

Results are results. What has happened since we have become involved in Quality Improvement? Are things getting better? Importantly, these good results should be tied directly to our approach and deployment. The Baldrige Award does not favor organizations who are just 'having a good year'. Rather, the Award seeks to recognize those organizations whose planning and implementation (approach and deployment) have generated real and tangible results.

The emphasis is on quantifiable results achieved over a number of years, normally three or more. What often surprises many applicants for the Baldrige Award is the need to compare our results to others in our industry, to the best in our industry, and to the best in the world. This type of aggressive benchmarking is a key component of Baldrige results. This approach to benchmarking is also very consistent with what we have recommended in *Making Quality Happen* – looking beyond our organization and being externally focused, not just regarding our customer measurements, but also regarding technologies, tools, and techniques that can help us continuously improve.

With each of our implementation actions we have been examining their relation to Baldrige Award criteria. These criteria provide a sound checklist to guarantee that we are not overlooking areas of particular importance. They should also be a continual reference point for our organization and particularly our Quality implementation team. This team should consider a regular self-assessment utilizing some of the Award criteria and then cross-referencing these self-assessment findings with a 'reality' check from our Quality council.

To any organization just undertaking Quality Improvement, these criteria may appear very daunting. However, they should be seen in perspective and a favorable self-assessment versus the Baldrige Award criteria – approach, deployment, and results – would represent where our organization should be approximately five years into our Quality Improvement efforts *if* the entire organization is really committing itself to real improvement and to the implementation of an honest cultural change.

SHORT-TERM QUALITY RESULTS

But what about short-term, what specifically should we be seeing after one or two years of implementing our Quality Improvement effort even as we remind ourselves that this process will not be accomplished in the first hundred days, nor the first thousand? We must begin our journey now and press forward, consistent with our attitude of continuous improvement. We will see results short-term and we will continuously improve if we concentrate on the basic 'blocking and tackling' implementation actions outlined in *Making Quality Happen*. These are the fundamentals of our Quality effort and they must be mastered and become second nature to our organization.

CUSTOMER FOCUS

Integral to all our implementation actions is a relentless focus on our customers, both internal and external. Regarding our customers, we must guard against becoming self-satisfied and content. Today's satisfied customer is not guaranteed to be there tomorrow. Many organizations make a great mistake in believing that their name and reputation alone will guarantee them a market. This is no longer true, not with worldwide competition and the numerous alternatives now being offered to our customers. Market share losses, reflecting this competition, have been precipitous in recent years, among

168

even the world's largest corporations, such as General Motors and International Business Machines. And just because our customers don't complain does not mean they are satisfied. Quite possibly our ineptitude has left them speechless!

COMMUNICATION AND PREVENTION

We have said that communication and prevention are the two key components of real Quality Improvement. These two elements should certainly be increasingly evident within our organization as we progress on our Quality journey. For example, we must continuously *communicate* with our customers. Constant contact with our customers will guarantee we never wake up one morning and find our market taken over by competition.

Tom Peters has remarked that a good indicator of our level of customer focus can be seen in our office 'in' box. Is our incoming office correspondence primarily focused on internal, organizational, or procedural matters? Peters' point is that perception is reality and if our customer is not in our daily correspondence and at the forefront of our attention, then they are nowhere. How often do we visit with customers, not to sell but to listen and learn? How often is our senior management with our customers? If they 'don't have the time', what are they spending their time on? And if we are not spending time with our customers, isn't it quite possible our competitors may be? Our management should be moving away from the reactive management style currently so characteristic of many industrial and service firms. Instead of waiting for new trends to overtake us, we must be actively working with our customers to continually address their changing needs and expectations.

In fact, it should be evident to our organization that we have an increasingly sharper picture of our customer and we should be continually seeking to develop an even more accurate means for determining their needs and expectations. We should be customer driven – driven to exceed our customers' expectations and driven to continually 'delight' them. We should be less and less interested in what our competitors are doing because our competitors should be viewing us as the technological and innovation leader, particularly as it regards our customers. Our goal should be to become the customer satisfaction benchmark, the best-in-class organization, not merely the best in our industry.

Additionally, we should be communicating more effectively *internally*. There should be fewer and fewer cases of organizational 'sibling rivalry' and more and more cross-functional teams working to eliminate existing problems and prevent future ones. In fact, functional lines should begin to disappear and the organization should increasingly see itself as one organization focused on our customers, rather than a series of separate fiefdoms, each with their own internally-focused goals and distinct, if not conflicting, agendas.

Our entire organization should be effectively communicating based upon its common language of Quality Improvement, starting with the vital employee–supervisor interface. All employees should be completely clear about the organization's objectives and goals, both short and long-term. Employees at all levels should be free to openly discuss with their supervisors problems, opportunities for improvement, and any other issue that relates to the success of the organization and our ability to better serve our customers. In fact, the lines between levels of management should gradually begin to blur, with employees empowered for greater and greater levels of responsibility. They should gain greater authority in supervising their own work and in assuming responsibility for their own measurement of Quality.

This is an organization moving more and more toward the world of prevention. The organization increasingly sees that everyone within it is responsible for Quality, not some third party such as Quality control or Quality assurance. These specific disciplines should be moving from inspection to a training and implementation function, particularly regarding our outside suppliers.

SUPPLIER PARTNERSHIPS

We must develop a clear understanding of needs and expectations, both with our customers and our suppliers. Remember, those supplying us cannot do so accurately, or 'right the first time', if we are unclear on what we desire from them. Importantly, these expectations are negotiated, not dictated.

It is particularly important that we begin to establish 'partnerships' with our outside suppliers. An important step in improving our relationship with our suppliers and developing a real partnership is our ability to begin negotiating expectations, based upon our supplier's input, skills, and capabilities. Our customer–supplier interface must become a two-way relationship based upon mutual profit, not punishment.

This type of relationship may be in sharp contrast to the traditionally adversarial one that we have historically employed. We need to bring our suppliers into a partnership where they are successful when we are successful, rather than a 'we win, you lose' situation. Specifically, if I know that I will be successful when the organization I supply is successful, then I will be working hard to guarantee that success, particularly if they let me.

It is amazing when one considers how often we keep suppliers at arm's length, never trusting them to become deeply involved in how their products or services are used within our organization. Yet, if our organization embraces our suppliers and makes them partners in our enterprise, we can draw upon their specific expertise for our benefit. Longer-term, these partnerships with our suppliers will be invaluable. They will enable our organization to focus more clearly on our processes, rather than policing suppliers, and will also enable us to deal with those 'certified' suppliers who have become actual partners in our success.

MANAGEMENT BY FACT

As we progress through the early years of our Quality journey, we should see broadscale use of measurement and the cost of non-Quality. Our organization should understand its key processes and begin to see important and significant improvement in each of them through measurement and the cost of non-Quality. We should be able to quantify these evolutionary steps in a variety of ways. First, we should see decreasing cycle times on all our key processes. This includes the cycle times for launching new products and services into the marketplace. How long does it take us now to get a new product to the market? Do we even know? How long to pay our bills?

How long before we are paid by our largest customers? If we had to put new advertising on air or in print immediately, just how soon would 'immediately' be? Moreover, we certainly need to examine and measure all the traditional cycle times for producing and delivering our goods and services.

We should see increasingly higher levels of customer satisfaction and decreasing levels of customer complaints, whether these complaints are about our products or services or about the delivery and payment for these products and services. We must continually remind ourselves that we are responsible for the entire transaction, no matter what that includes, even if we are not the ones who finally set up or deliver our product or service. The product or service invariably will have our name on it, and therefore the customer will be looking to us, not some faceless, nameless middleman.

If we use distributors, it is vitally important that we understand how they are perceived by our mutual customers. They are our interface with the eventual customer and we should be very clear just how well they are representing us. It is not enough to content ourselves with an examination of our relationship with these distributors. We must be completely confident about their interaction with the final customer, because if they fail in that interaction, we fail also.

Customer input is key, whether about a distributor we use or about our organization directly. Many organizations have 800 (free call) telephone numbers for receiving customer input. Data received by these 800 numbers can provide very useful customer information – what percentage of total calls are negative, what is the trend, what are the top ten complaints, are we addressing them? However, is our only measure of customer satisfaction based upon the number of customer complaints? If so, this provides a very limited, ill-defined image of customer satisfaction and certainly not the proactive one we should be embracing.

Therefore, we should be examining some type of ongoing market research that keeps our fingers on the pulse of our customers and those who currently are not utilizing our product or service, but could be. It is important to remember that our own employees are an invaluable resource in this regard, since many of them are in direct contact with our customers every day. Therefore our employees should be our first source of customer satisfaction information and detail.

With a clearer understanding of our customer and a healthier, mutually beneficial relationship with our suppliers, we should be seeing an ever increasing accuracy level in our forecasting of customer demand. Previously, if we missed a month's forecast we were a failure. However, if we exceeded forecast, we wore the hero's laurels. Unfortunately each scenario was really a miss because each caused problems to those producing our product or services.

In the case of the down-side miss, we pay a penalty in excess inventory. On the up side, when we exceed the forecast, we have unfilled customer orders, the potential for dissatisfied customers, and quite often lost market share. Therefore, with better communication with our customers and suppliers – sometimes even in the form of electronic data interfaces – we should be seeing consistently less variability in our forecast versus actual levels.

A directly related measurement of Quality Improvement progress for our organization is that inventories should be continually declining. This means all levels of inventory, including raw material, work in process, and finished goods. These declines occur as we continually increase our understanding of our customer. Armed with a clearer understanding of their needs and expectations – not only of the actual product or service, but of the delivery, timing, and other service features that accompany almost every product and service – we are better able to forecast our customer's demands. Additionally, our partnership relationship with suppliers will enable our organization to develop relationships based in Quality, lowest delivered cost, delivery schedule, and possibly even geographic location – are they around the block or around the globe? – thereby eliminating the need for 'just-in-case' inventories in favor of 'just-in-time' inventories.

With improved forecasting and a clearer understanding of our customer, our order-fill rates should be moving closer and closer to 100%. Surprisingly, many organizations have an accepted standard for filling customers' orders at less than 100%. Many organizations are completely satisfied with filling only 70% of a customer's order. How would we feel about that fill rate if our supermarkets adopted a similar attitude: 'sorry, we can only sell you eight eggs, not a full

173

dozen and you'll have to put back two cans from that six-pack'? Because we now have the same standards for our personal and business lives, we know that this is unacceptable. We now have one standard, one attitude, and because we are committed to continuous improvement, we should be seeing our order rates steadily improving. This is an exact reflection of our closer and closer relationship with our customer and our clearer and clearer understanding of their needs and expectations.

Additionally, our product and service costs should be declining as our employees continually provide input on how our processes can be improved and our profit margins increased. Moreover, our organizational or administrative costs as a percent of total sales should also be declining as our productivity levels increase. This is a reflection of our needing fewer and fewer employees to do the rework, checking, inspecting, sorting, counting, and shifting that are currently so predominant in our organization. We will not be eliminating these people, merely the type of work they used to do. They will now be used more productively to actually produce our goods and services, to 'add value' rather than merely 'adding cost' to our processes.

Moreover, because our productivity levels are increasing, we should be able to break out of the continual 'down-sizing' syndrome which has ensnared so many organizations. While we should not see headcount levels increasing, they should at least stabilize. This provides our organization with some sense of security and lets them concentrate on their jobs and improving their process, rather than concentrating on the latest rumor.

BENCHMARKING

Benchmarking should be an increasingly visible element in all our functions. Benchmarking entails measuring our processes against the best at that function, from any industry. As we stated in Chapter 7, benchmarking is key to improving our measures, once we understand our own processes. We should know what the industry leaders are achieving in each of our functions and we should be striving to meet and exceed these levels. We should be making these important gains with direct input and contributions from our organization,

174

and specifically from those directly involved with each process, our involved and empowered employees.

For example, our customer service group should determine what organization has the best customer service levels, after they have documented their own process. Then they should compare our process to this industry leading benchmark. This is entirely consistent with our Continuous Improvement attitude on Quality.

Importantly, benchmarking should not be confused with working to industry 'standards' or averages. 'We're at the industry standard, so we're okay.' That is just another refrain from the 'If it ain't broke, don't fix it' songbook. Industry standards are changing daily, possibly hourly. If we're not leading that change then we're following and the 1990s will not be the decade of the successful follower.

Therefore, each of our functional areas should be developing benchmarks for our key functions or processes. This is probably the process we have already begun measuring. Now we are merely adding a comparative element to that measure – how are we doing versus the best? Are we the Gold Medalist in our respective disciplines or the novice? Longer term, we should not be content until we are the benchmark. That is the real goal of benchmarking.

CORRECTIVE ACTION

Corrective action should be a natural extension of measurement and the cost of non-Quality, so that once we know how often problems occur and what they are costing us, we should be moving to prioritize them for permanent elimination. Again, corrective action should always take place at the earliest possible stage, at the lowest possible level within the organization. Only major, organization-wide problems should be brought to management for resolution. Empower our workforce and they will identify and eliminate existing problems. It is management's role to do the empowering and to be proactive so that future problems are prevented. They are able to do this by listening to the organization, not dictating to it.

These are some of the elements we should be seeing during the first years of our Quality journey. However, the championship athlete does not review the basic fundamentals of their sport during the actual event. There isn't time. These fundamentals must become ingrained in their performance through days, weeks, months, and even years of practice, practice, practice. The same is exactly true for our quest for Quality Improvement. We must be focused.

FOCUS

We focus first by living the basic concepts of Quality, with special emphasis on prevention and continuous improvement achieved through effective communication. These concepts are already part of our personal life, now we need to make them an integral part of our organizational culture. These concepts cannot be short-cut. There are no easy ways out. There is no such thing as 'situational Quality'. Just as real weight loss or blood pressure control involve a lifestyle change, so will our commitment to Quality.

We must remember that our organization will be watching our every action, particularly at the outset. This is particularly true for every manager and anyone in any supervisory role, with no exceptions. Action is the operative word because the organization is conditioned to hearing (and discarding) a lot from management. They are now looking for the actions that support those words.

SHARPEN OUR FOCUS

We sharpen this focus by looking for successes and celebrating them. We discussed recognition in Chapter 10, but this celebration of success must extend to the basic supervisor–employee relationship. It must become a mentoring relationship, with the supervisor taking pride in – and receiving recognition for – developing those who report to them. When this climate permeates our entire organization, we will see distinct improvement and real team progress. If

176

our organization currently has a 'supervisor as cop' mentality, then we must address this key issue at the outset. We will not be able to make significant improvement until our supervisors assume the role of 'examples, helpers, and advocates' and relinquish their role as 'police'.

TIGHTEN OUR FOCUS

We tighten our focus by continually improving our Quality Improvement efforts by attacking and improving specific, prioritized, and narrowly defined processes. Our Quality process must continuously improve, along with every other process within our organization. However, it is important to guard against rapid or sudden jumps in our Quality process. Rather, we should seek gradual refinements and improvements. Our Quality council is an excellent vehicle for informing us concerning what is and is not working in our implementation plan.

All of these changes should begin to appear within the first one to two years, depending upon the size of the organization. They should not be long in appearing if we have established a solid approach and provided a fertile environment for their growth. It is particularly important during this initial period that we maintain close ties with our Quality council to accurately gauge the real progress of our Quality Improvement efforts. We should not be afraid to make minor adjustments. Further, there should be no pride in authorship should one part of our process need any type of reworking. We must continually remind ourselves that we will succeed ultimately when the Quality Improvement efforts we have developed succeed in achieving our organizational objectives. But it will depend on each of us to do our part and more. We are the ones who will benefit and therefore we must be the ones making Quality happen.

Epilogue: Continuous improvement

12

Rapid jumps or course changes in our process will disrupt our focus. Quick fixes and miracle cures are not what we need for making Quality happen. There are currently a multitude of Quality acronyms being presented as the latest panacea by their exponents. Several organizations already embarked on a Quality effort have begun jumping from one acronym program to another, thereby completely confusing their organizations that had been focusing on the basic principles of Quality Improvement – the basic blocking and tackling we have already discussed.

Our approach to new developments and techniques should be an evolutionary one. If they are practicable, they should be blended into our existing effort. Remember our emphasis on making Quality an integral part of our organization. It must be seen as part of the natural order of our organization. Therefore, refinements to the process must be treated as natural evolutions of our basic process rather than as radical departures. We are looking for continuous improvement from any source possible. However, we do not want a 'flavor of the month' approach to continuous improvement.

Some of the Quality acronyms currently in vogue include: SPC (statistical process control); TEI (total employee involvement); QFD (quality function deployment); BPQM (business process quality management); JIT ('just in time'); and TQM (total quality management). Let's examine each of these items and determine what they really mean, and, if useful, how they may already be part of our

Quality process or can be easily assimilated into our process for making quality happen.

SPC – STATISTICAL PROCESS CONTROL

Statistical process control really should not be considered even remotely faddish. It is only discussed under this heading because a number of consultants are presenting SPC to various organizations as an 'end-all, be-all' for Quality. Clearly, SPC is not an end but a means to an end – that end is the achievement of our organization's objectives. SPC is a strategic tool we should be using to assist us in that process. SPC is not *the* process and we will not achieve any type of real Quality Improvement by utilizing only SPC. Rather, it should be a natural extension of our measurement efforts, which are already in integral part of our Quality Improvement plan.

SPC has appeared faddish because shockingly large parts of American and European organizations do not use this basic business tool developed in the 1920s. Moreover, in organizations where SPC is used, it is invariably confined to the 'manufacturing ghetto' and not seen as applicable to sales, marketing, research and development, or finance. In fact, it is applicable across our entire organization, wherever we are measuring.

We discussed in Chapter 6 that all work is a process and therefore we can measure aspects of that process, particularly the degree to which we meet or exceed our customers' needs and expectations. If we can measure that process, then we should be able to apply SPC to it as well. How can we tell if a process is really producing what our customers want on a consistent basis without statistical measurement?

Let's examine two non-manufacturing examples. Marketing is responsible for developing the organization's forecast – the forecast that drives many other functions within the organization, most notably sales and manufacturing. Yet, despite the great importance of the forecast as a business planning tool, few organizations really monitor how well they forecast beyond the 'over forecast – good' and 'under forecast – bad' mentality. This is an excellent opportunity to use SPC to determine if our fore-cast process is in control, or more likely, completely out of control.

SPC should enable us to see, over time, continuous improvement in forecasting because we are now going to be examining the elements that make up our forecasting model in far greater detail. As we better understand these elements – seasonality, inventories (our's and our customer's), weather, and many other variables – we will see our forecast performance improve and we can see that most clearly through our SPC measurements. So our forecasting process is a natural candidate for SPC.

An important theme throughout this book has been the necessity for focusing on our customers and continually improving how we serve them. Many organizations have extensive customer-service groups that handle consumer inquiries, complaints, and compliments. Increasingly, we find '800' (free call) telephone numbers available to consumers to facilitate this communication.

Yet, what are we really doing with the data these centers collect? Are we making use of the information by tracking positive and negative responses by appropriate categories – such as complaints/compliments by product? And do we know where all these trends are headed over time, or do we just have a 'warm, fuzzy' feeling? King Kong could give us a warm, fuzzy feeling too, so we had better take proactive charge of our customer data and SPC is an ideal way for doing this.

We can clearly track, over time, our customer complaint trends with SPC and take action before major problems occur. We can do this by spotting developing trends instead of waiting for the 'Challengers' and 'Titanics' that occur when we merely react to circumstances around us. With SPC, we can pinpoint the most significant areas of customer input and act accordingly. Best of all, we are now armed with clear, concise, quantitative data about our customer service operation, not just feelings about it.

In conclusion, SPC should be seen as a powerful tool that all parts of our organization should be implementing and making full use of and it is a natural extension of the measurement process we have already established.

TEI – TOTAL EMPLOYEE INVOLVEMENT

Many organizations have become enthralled with the concept of TEI after reading Tom Peters and observing Baldrige Award winning companies such as Milliken, Federal Express, and Xerox. These Quality leadership organizations place great emphasis on employee participation, as we have already discussed. Organizations wishing to follow in such sizeable footsteps are now trying to develop their own TEI programs as an organizational 'add-on' rather than as part of their basic operation. Many times these programs are preceded by a survey of employees on a variety of work related subjects. Numerous consultants are offering the ideal TEI survey to initiate such programs.

Invariably these surveys portray concerns employees have with management – lack of clear direction, seemingly capricious changes in objectives, short-term orientation, poor internal communication. These are just a sample of typical employee responses, regardless of industry. However, management becomes uncomfortable when these results are examined and invariably seeks to refocus the survey results back on employees and their shortcomings rather than those of management. In many instances management does this by forming employee teams to develop corrective actions for the identified problems or related issues. Of course, these corrective action recommendations are uncomfortable for employees to develop and impractical, if not impossible, to implement because they involve employee concerns about management's basic operating style, over which the employees have no control.

Therefore, this type of employee involvement 'program' churns up a great deal of time, money, and effort while producing zero in real employee involvement. In fact, the results of such ill-conceived efforts are many times worse than the original situation they sought to address. Quite often employees see that their real concerns, which were honestly presented, are not being addressed. Rather, management seeks to focus the program on the employees and away from the organization's real problems which are management driven. This leaves employees embittered and with a very negative feeling towards any future TEI efforts.

Quality circles were an example of this type of misdirected TEI program in the 1960s and 1970s. These 'circles' featured teams of employees making specific recommendations to management on improving various processes. Because management was not directly involved in these circles at the outset, and participated only when final recommendations were made by these groups, management was invariably on the defensive and more often than not vetoed the recommendations. This killed any effectiveness Quality circles could have had and they expired in the US and much of Europe as just another Quality and employee involvement 'fad'.

Instead of developing a new process or program for TEI, we need to include this basic idea of improved internal communication as an integral part of our basic Quality Improvement effort. Clearly, employee involvement is a primary part of our corrective action efforts detailed in Chapter 8. We recommend that employees identify problems and assist in eliminating them. Further, we want to develop a culture where the basic employee–supervisor interface is an open and honest one. This is an enormous first step towards real employee involvement. A sound employee–supervisor interface will promote the sharing of ideas and represent a real opportunity for employee involvement within our current organizational structure, rather than foisting some new external program on the organization.

One way to make employee involvement a natural part of our organization is to recognize employee teams making important contributions to achieving our organization's objectives, as we discussed in Chapter 10. Once management begins publicly recognizing employees for their contributions, the rest of the organization will quickly assimilate this learning and act accordingly – what gets recognized gets repeated. We will then have real TEI and it will be viewed by the organization as a natural part of our daily business regimen.

QFD – QUALITY FUNCTION DEPLOYMENT

QFD provides an in-depth and detailed process for determining customer needs and expectations and prioritizing them by utilizing a hierarchical matrix. In this book, we have previously defined Quality as 'meeting or exceeding customer needs and expectations'

(p. 24) so there is nothing wrong with trying to better understand our customers and their needs and expectations. In fact, the entire theme of this book is to be externally focused and proactive concerning our customers. Any tool that can help us do that should be used.

However, we should make certain that any tool we select does not replace direct interaction with our customers. No matrix or hierarchical rankings should replace face-to-face discussions with our customers. Further, an effective tool need not be overly complicated to be useful. Process mapping and the process model we discussed in Chapter 6 are basic tools for identifying and dealing with customer needs and expectations. We need to be comfortable with these basics before we jump to new tools. We need to solo first before we move to supersonic jet qualification.

In dealing with customer needs and expectations we already have a very powerful weapon in our existing arsenal, yet one which is often neglected – Market Research. Well executed market research can give us invaluable insight into the wants, needs, habits, and practices of our customers. Armed with this information, we can then present them product or service alternatives through additional market research studies.

Often, organizations are limited in their market research applications because of their limited knowledge, or imagination, when the subject of research arises. This is the market research paradigm. We often equate market research solely with the mindless election polls we hear so much about prior to our biannual trips to the voting booth. These election polls are usually poorly executed, conducted by one political party to further their particular cause, and in general do more harm than good to the reputation of the market research industry.

However, very sophisticated consumer research techniques exist and more are appearing each year. These techniques can give us hard, quantitative data on the needs and expectations of our customers and can do so very economically. Techniques featuring voice pitch analysis, galvanic skin response, and eye tracking can each provide key insight into exactly what our customers really want, to the point of answering everyone's most important question, 'would you buy this?'

184

QFD may appear to be an external solution when we have the means of addressing customer needs and expectations within our own organization. We need to be qualified and competent in our existing arsenal and utilize our market research expertise as we examine the application of QFD. Good, innovative, and imaginative market research can play an invaluable role in assisting us with our customers and their needs and expectations. We should take every opportunity to meet with these customers and speak with them, first hand. If hierarchical matrices can help us towards that end, fine, but we must always remind ourselves that this is another strategic tool for our arsenal, not an end or an objective in itself.

BPQM – BUSINESS PROCESS QUALITY MANAGEMENT

BPQM addresses the business processes which make up our organization. This technique for Quality Improvement is targeted at identifying and delineating these processes, determining those responsible for them (process owners) and then determining which processes need corrective action for improvement or problem elimination.

The entire thought process underlying BPQM is sound and its basis is the process mapping we covered in Chapter 6. Our organization's problems stem from process problems, not people problems, as we have previously discussed. Additionally, an organization would do itself an enormous benefit if it would take the time to clearly delineate the process flow of its major business processes. Specifically, where does a specific process start and where does it end? Who is responsible for managing this process – who is the process owner? What is the output of this process and who is the customer for this output? And do we know what our customer wants this output to look like – do we know the customer's needs and expectations?

In a surprisingly large number of cases we will not have the answers to these very basic questions. We will have an answer, sometimes based upon assumptions, sometimes based upon historical practice, but many times developed entirely without input from the customer of our process. Additionally, we will often find that even our most basic business processes are not clearly defined and are not easily diagrammed in even the most rudimentary fashion.

For example, a major advertising agency was asked to select one of their major processes for an exercise in process flow diagramming. The process selected was 'developing a direct mail advertising piece'. Since this advertising agency did a great deal of business in the direct mail area and prided itself on its expertise in this field, this was an excellent example to examine. However, the agency personnel involved in the exercise soon discovered that they could not neatly diagram the process of developing a direct mail advertising piece. To their horror, there was not one clear 'start to finish' process. Instead, it was a process that meandered throughout the agency based on the whims of various departments, the availability of certain individuals, and the person responsible for the account.

Clearly, the agency had been somewhat successful in the direct mail advertising business, but they quickly came to the conclusion that every direct mail advertising project had been handled as if it had been the agency's first ever. There was no clear process, there were no process owners, and there were no clear procedures. What they had was the blueprint for a disaster and the exercise of diagramming this basic business process enabled them to see this and begin work to establish a clear process flow and ownership.

Throughout *Making Quality Happen* we have stressed the need to examine processes. In Chapter 6 we detailed how the key elements of process flow and process management should be an integral part of our Quality training program and therefore an important part of our Quality Improvement effort. With these elements as an integral part of our basic Quality Improvement effort, there is no need to add on BPQM.

There is absolutely nothing wrong with the principles underlying BPQM. In fact, this technique was developed by an organization because it discovered, as an afterthought, that its Quality Improvement effort was not addressing the key organization processes and therefore its Quality Improvement effort was not having a major impact. Instead of addressing the major processes, this organization's Quality Improvement effort was promoting improvement in smaller, department level projects.

186

Clearly, there is nothing wrong with improvement at any level, except that management was not seeing the level and extent of improvement that they had originally envisioned. Part of the problem was that management had not directly involved itself in the improvement process. In this regard, an important first step is for management to identify its view of the organization's key processes. Currently existing problems in these processes should be addressed immediately and methods for continually improving these processes should be sought from those directly involved in them.

Thereafter, each part of our organization should identify and delineate its key processes, with particular emphasis on those processes where problems are occurring. This should be a key part of our Quality Improvement effort from the outset. This is an important way of making Quality a natural part of our normal work environment and not something added on. BPQM was developed as an add-on to the basic Quality Improvement effort because its originators had not been process driven from the outset. There is no need for our organization to repeat their mistakes, rather we should learn from them for our benefit.

JIT – JUST IN TIME

JIT is a perfect addition to this discussion of Quality Improvement acronyms in that it shares a variety of common elements with our previously discussed items. To start with JIT is frequently considered a 'hot, new' concept based upon 'Japanese management principles'. It is also seen as confined to the manufacturing ghetto, and in this context, is many times referred to as 'just in time inventory'. Finally, it is often viewed as another program which must be imported to our organization and which, because of its complicated nature, will require extensive training – and therefore be doomed to failure.

In fact, all of these notions are incorrect. The concepts underlying JIT are quite fundamental to the Quality Improvement effort we have outlined in *Making Quality Happen* and are already in place and waiting for duty in our 'process oriented' improvement effort. For our purposes, we believe the traditional definition of JIT as 'a

187

process of continuous improvement dedicated to the progressive elimination of all non valued-added work' is appropriate. This definition makes the JIT concepts completely consistent with everything we have recommended for our Quality Improvement effort.

Importantly, JIT is not new and is certainly not a Japanese import. Like SPC, JIT is an American business principle that has grown dusty from non-use in the US while the Japanese have honed it to razor sharpness in their bid to dominate world industry. The basic principles of JIT were an integral part of Henry Ford's original assembly line and are based on the easily understood premise that 'time is money' and that elements that waste time in our process should be removed.

Additionally, while JIT is often confined to manufacturing in those few organizations even attempting to utilize it, the principles have significant applications throughout our organization. We need to return to our basic premise that all work is a process and that this process produces an output that goes to a customer by transforming or employing various inputs that come from suppliers. Our concepts of process flow and process management help us see the scope of the process and where problems, or potential problems, exist. Our overriding attitude of Quality – continuous improvement – requires that we continually seek to improve our process and that is exactly what JIT is all about. Our process can be anywhere within an organization – writing a marketing plan, preparing a budget, making a presentation, conducting an experiment, repairing a machine. Each involves a process and each of these processes can be improved, particularly concerning the time element.

Because JIT deals with these basic business areas, we can also put to rest the belief that JIT will require extensive and complicated training which must be imported. In fact, JIT is one of the simplest, most easily understood principles in Quality Improvement – so basic that even our management will understand it, if we speak slowly and use small words!

What we need to explain is that time is money and increasingly organizations are competing on time. How long does it take to get a product to market, how long does it take us to get a New Drug Application approved for the Food and Drug Administration, how long does it take to transport 400 000 men and women to the

188

Middle East? Time is the essence of business, not because those who are first necessarily win, but because time represents a cost we have direct control over and can do something about. What we can do about time is directly proportional to how creative and imaginative we are. JIT is a process that rewards these very rare qualities of creativity and imagination.

Let's look at a basic process we have already discussed in this chapter – developing a direct mail advertising piece. We have already diagrammed this process for a process flow and with process management we have identified current and potential problem areas. Now we can add time to the process. Just how long does this process take from start to finish – what is the cycle time? How long does each step within the process take? What steps in the process really add value and which merely add time and therefore add cost?

We add value when we actually do something to the product or service. In our example, developing the artwork, creating the media plan, obtaining the mailing list, and actually mailing the item are all value adding actions. We add cost when we wait or add time to the process. For example, when we wait for legal clearance for the text of the advertisement, when we store the direct mail pieces before shipping them to the post office, when we wait for an appointment with our management to review the concept with them. All these items add time, lengthen our process cycle time, and therefore add cost to our process. JIT strives to eliminate these dollar drains by shortening cycle times. We accomplish this by challenging each step in our process and continuously improving each one.

The fundamentals of JIT are ideally suited for inclusion into our Quality Improvement process orientation. We do not need to 'add on' JIT at some later date, but can make it a part of our effort from the outset, as part of our continuous improvement attitude of Quality. Many organizations have completed their Quality training efforts and then focused their employees on their business processes and challenged the organization to improve these processes by eliminating existing problems and by striving to continuously improve them by adding value and cutting time and costs. This provides the organization with a direct application of their Quality training and provides clear direction for making Quality happen. That is why the JIT concept is integral to our Chapter 6 discussion – 'if they learn only one thing'.

TQM – TOTAL QUALITY MANAGEMENT

The term 'total Quality management' is often used as an umbrella for a series of Quality related initiatives which are combined under one 'TQM' heading. Many organizations – probably dominated by engineers – have even gone to the extent of expressing TQM as an equation made up of various other Quality acronyms. For example,

$$TQM = TEI + QIP + BPQM + JIT$$

This sounds nice and even looks very thorough, but can leave us with the feeling that maybe we have left something out of the equation, particularly if we are not good at math to begin with.

Still other organizations present TQM as a series of stages an organization passes through. One approach says that the first stage is obtaining conformance from your internal processes – do they produce what they are supposed to 'right the first time'. The next phase introduces the customer into the process and the organization then adapts their process to the customer's needs and expectations. A third phase shifts attention to the competition and beating them through superior quality. Other phases follow, but this TQM approach gives the impression of opening one of those Russian dolls. Each time we open one, there is another, slightly smaller doll inside, which we open to discover yet another doll, etc.

Both of these two approaches to TQM overly complicate what is a very basic and easily understood subject, which this book has sought to further simplify rather than complicate.

Quality is not some puzzle with a series of parts which we first must find and then must all fit together just so. Neither is Quality a rite of passage where we move from one stage to another as we learn new 'secrets'. The whole problem with the Quality cottage industry that has sprung up and begun spouting new acronyms is that it has taken a very simple, basic, and intuitively obvious concept – people want to do good work and receive what they were promised – and made it excruciatingly complicated. Quality Improvement and our process for achieving it should not become brain surgery by mail! If it does not make sense, if it is not logical, then it should be questioned, examined, and rethought.

190

Quality Improvement is often presented in this complicated guise to senior management by the Quality cottage industry because why else would management not have seen the wisdom of this concept earlier? The answer lies in the fact that we are all too comfortable with the here and now, with what we know, with 'the way it's always been done'. This keeps us from examining the new and the different until we are forced by circumstances to do so.

In *Making Quality Happen* we have seen that Quality and Quality Improvement are really natural extensions of our personal standards and practices. There is nothing radically new to be learned, but rather old, established beliefs that need to be remembered and relearned. Shouldn't we really provide what our customers want instead of just what we can produce? Isn't it better to plan ahead for events rather than waiting for them to overtake and overwhelm us? Aren't 'two heads better than one' and therefore aren't a thousand excited and contributing employees more likely to improve our operation than ten homogeneous management board memnbers? Don't we always want to do things better and better and don't we really want to know how much better we're getting rather than having to guess about our progress?

So now we begin our Quality Improvement journey. *Making Quality Happen* has tried to illuminate some of the shadowy parts of the adventure and point out the potential pitfalls, but we must take the lead and, with our objectives clear and ever before us, go about making Quality happen.

191

Index

Page numbers appearing in **bold** refer to figures